Lawns

YOUR QUICK GUIDE TO A BEAUTIFUL YARD

Contents

Meredith® Books
Des Moines, Iowa

Scotts Lawns
Editor: Alrica Goldstein
Contributing Editor: Megan McConnell Hughes
Writers: Dr. Nick E. Christians, Ashton Ritchie
Copy Chief: Terri Fredrickson
Publishing Operations Manager: Karen Schirm
Senior Editor, Asset and Information Manager:
    Phillip Morgan
Edit and Design Production Coordinator: Mary Lee Gavin
Editorial Assistant: Kathleen Stevens
Book Production Managers: Pam Kvitne,
    Marjorie J. Schenkelberg, Rick von Holdt, Mark Weaver
Contributing Proofreaders: Wendy Polhemus-Annibell,
    Terri Krueger, Barb Rothfus
Indexer: Ellen Davenport Sherron

**Additional Editorial Contributions from
Art Rep Services**
Director: Chip Nadeau
Illustrator: Michael Surles

Meredith® Books
Executive Director, Editorial: Gregory H. Kayko
Executive Director, Design: Matt Strelecki
Managing Editor: Amy Tincher-Durik
Executive Editor/Group Manager: Benjamin W. Allen
Senior Associate Design Director: Tom Wegner
Marketing Product Manager: Isaac Petersen

Publisher and Editor in Chief: James D. Blume
Editorial Director: Linda Raglan Cunningham
Executive Director, New Business Development:
    Todd M. Davis
Executive Director, Sales: Ken Zagor
Director, Operations: George A. Susral
Director, Production: Douglas M. Johnston
Director, Marketing: Amy Nichols
Business Director: Jim Leonard

Vice President and General Manager: Douglas J. Guendel

Meredith Publishing Group
President: Jack Griffin
Executive Vice President: Bob Mate

Meredith Corporation
Chairman and Chief Executive Officer: William T. Kerr
President and Chief Operating Officer: Stephen M. Lacy

In Memoriam: E.T. Meredith III (1933-2003)

All of us at Meredith® Books are dedicated to providing you with the information and ideas you need to enhance your home and garden. We welcome your comments and suggestions about this book. Write to us at:
    Meredith Corporation
    Meredith Gardening Books
    1716 Locust St.
    Des Moines, IA 50309-3023

If you would like more information on Scotts products, call 800/543-TURF or visit us at: www.scotts.com

Roundup® is a registered trademark of The Monsanto Company and it's affiliates.

Note to the Readers: Due to differing conditions, tools, and individual skills, Meredith Corporation assumes no responsibility for any damages, injuries suffered, or losses incurred as a result of following the information published in this book. Before beginning any project, review the instructions carefully, and if any doubts or questions remain, consult local experts or authorities. Because codes and regulations vary greatly, you always should check with authorities to ensure that your project complies with all applicable local codes and regulations. Always read and observe all of the safety precautions provided by manufacturers of any tools, equipment, or supplies, and follow all accepted safety procedures.

Introduction

L awns have long been a source of pride for families. It's hard to match the feeling of accomplishment that comes from looking out the front door at a beautiful green carpet of grass or from watching children play on cool, soft turf or knowing that your efforts enhance the value and beauty of your neighborhood and community.

Lawn care isn't difficult and doesn't need to be expensive. With a little knowledge, a sense of timing, and the helpful hints provided on the following pages, even beginners can achieve results that will have the neighbors seeking their advice.

In this book it's easy to find answers quickly. The first four chapters address day-to-day tips for caring for your lawn. Fertilizing, watering, mowing, and managing thatch and compaction are all covered. Next you'll find a troubleshooting chapter to aide you in addressing any lawn problems and finally you'll find a section all about reviving your lawn. Begin creating and caring for your dream lawn today.

Lawns make the world cooler and quieter and form the perfect backdrop for a backyard retreat.

Benefits
of a lawn

A single blade of grass may not seem very impressive. However, when joined by the millions of blades in a lawn, it is part of an incredibly diverse and active ecosystem that benefits homeowners and society alike.

A vigorous, healthy lawn can increase property value and is known to affect how we respond to the world around us. Most people say that the best place to relax is in their own backyard.

Well-maintained lawns provide truly marvelous environmental benefits as well. Consider just a few of the ways that healthy grass forms a vital link in the environmental chain society depends on.

■ *Cooler and quieter:* When the heat is on, grass helps keep you cool. Street or sidewalk temperatures may reach 100°F or higher, but grass remains at a pleasant 75°F, cooling nearby living areas. Grass also makes your life a bit quieter. It effectively absorbs and deflects sound.

■ *Help in breathing:* A healthy lawn is an amazingly efficient production system. Grass plants remove carbon dioxide from the air and produce oxygen in return.

■ *Soil saver:* Grass controls erosion by knitting the soil together, trapping runoff water, and eliminating many of the problems caused by dust and mud. And it's one of the more efficient water savers you'll find in nature. A healthy lawn absorbs rainfall six times more effectively than a wheat field.

■ *Pollution fighter:* In one year's time, the blades and roots in an acre of healthy grass absorb hundreds of pounds of pollutants from the air and rainwater. A common misconception is that the products put on lawns contribute to groundwater contamination and to algae blooms in nearby ponds and lakes. The truth is that few materials get past grass roots. The dense root system under a healthy lawn captures pollutants as water filters through the soil.

■ *Safe surface:* Perhaps the most important benefit is the recreational value lawns provide for young and old. Dense turf is a safer playground and playing field than nearly any other surface.

Fertilizing

Fertilizer
basics

To provide optimal growth, split the total amount of fertilizer required annually into three to five applications.

A healthy lawn is a feast for the eyes. It is thick and luxurious and has luscious color. No empty spaces offer a home for weeds. The blades are strong, the roots dense and far-spreading. The key to such health and beauty? Good nutrition on a regular schedule.

Grass grows constantly, which means it requires a steady diet of nutrients. Even though many nutrients occur naturally in soil, the soil is unable to supply them as fast as or in the quantities that the plants call for them. For that reason, good nutrition for a lawn is the result of a balanced fertilizer program that supplies the right nutrients in the correct amounts at the best time for the lawn.

The ideal fertilizer program is one that provides uniform growth throughout the season. Most fertilizers have the details figured out for you on the label.

QUALITY

Lawns will survive without fertilizer. However, the less fertilizer the lawn receives, the more its quality deteriorates. As a lawn runs out of nutrients, the first thing to go is color. The luscious green turns pale. Over time, the lawn thins. Thin spots provide space for weeds to move in. Deficient grass is not vigorous, and if diseases and insects attack, it cannot outgrow damage.

Although it's true that the more fertilizer a lawn receives the better it looks, overfertilizing can be bad too. Overfertilizing stimulates leaf growth at the expense of the roots. The root system will be thin and shallow, so the lawn can't stand up to heat or drought. The succulent shoots are easy prey for diseases and insects. In addition, overfertilizing promotes thatch.

A MATTER OF BALANCE

As a general rule, lawns in northern regions, called cool-season lawns, should receive three to five feedings per year. Most lawns in southern regions, known as warm-season lawns, require three to six, depending on how many months they actively grow.

The number of feedings listed here provide for a lawn of the highest quality. Several conditions can alter these general recommendations. For example, some grasses such as centipedegrass and buffalograss do best with less fertilizer. In areas with very sandy soil, a lawn may need more frequent feeding. Bottomline—applying the proper amount of fertilizer for your conditions will result in a lawn with fewer weed, insect, and disease problems.

WHEN TO FERTILIZE

It's best to split the total amount of fertilizer required annually into three to five applications. The timing of the feedings and the amount you apply with each one depends on whether your lawn is a cool- or warm-season species. In general it is best to fertilize when the lawn is actively growing, when fertilizer will enhance root growth and food storage.

Cool-season grasses put on the most growth during spring and fall. During the summer, growth slows as the grass waits out the heat. When temperatures cool in fall, the lawn resumes growth, but now it is storing food for the winter ahead.

For cool-season grasses, then, the biggest feedings should be in late summer and fall. Provide two meals, one in late summer to thicken the stand and grow healthy roots. A second feeding a month or so later winterizes the lawn to build food reserves for the dormant period ahead. Spring calls for small snacks in early and late spring.

The growing calendar for warm-season grasses is opposite that for cool-season grasses. Warm-season grasses sit still during cool months and grow steadily from midspring to early fall. Provide warm-season grasses with several small meals all summer.

The exact date to fertilize depends on your location. In Houston the first round of fertilizer may go down in March, but in Minneapolis the first chance to fertilize might be late April. As a guide, time the first feeding to coincide with the first mowing. You know the grass is growing then.

How the grasses rank

NEEDS THE MOST FEEDING
- Bermudagrass
- Kentucky bluegrass

- Zoysiagrass
- Perennial ryegrass
- St. Augustinegrass
- Tall fescue

- Fine fescues
- Bahiagrass

- Centipedegrass
- Buffalograss

NEEDS THE LEAST FEEDING

Types of *fertilizer*

Don't let the many different types of fertilizer intimidate you. Armed with basic knowledge about fertilizer analysis, nitrogen sources, and fertilizer form, you'll choose the best product for your lawn. Read the label, set the spreader to the specified setting, and you're ready to go.

UNDERSTANDING LABELS

Federal and state laws require that all fertilizer labels supply the same information. Once you know the code, reading a label is a cinch.

■ *The analysis:* First, all fertilizer packages display three numbers—the fertilizer's analysis. The analysis refers to three essential nutrients: nitrogen, phosphorus, and potassium. Each number stands for the percent of the package made up of the available form of each nutrient by weight. The analysis shows the nutrients as a ratio to one another. For example, a 29-3-4 fertilizer has approximately a 10-1-1 ratio.

How do you compare two fertilizers with the same analysis ratio? Look at the pounds of nitrogen delivered per thousand square feet and the source of the nitrogen.

To convert the analysis to pounds of nitrogen, multiply the package weight by the percentage of nitrogen. For example, a typical 15½-pound bag of 29-3-4 holds 4½ pounds of nitrogen (15½ × 29%). Divide that number by the number of 1,000-square-foot units the bag covers—5 for the 5,000 square-foot coverage of a 15½-pound bag—and you learn that 29-3-4 fertilizer supplies 9/10 pound of nitrogen per 1,000 square feet (4½ pounds ÷ 5).

The available forms of phosphorus and potassium are P_2O_5 and K_2O. Determining their actual amounts in a fertilizer is less straightforward and rarely necessary.

■ *Nitrogen source:* Fertilizers are either fast- or slow-release or a combination of the two. The lawn doesn't care which you use; the end nitrogen product is the same. However, you will notice differences in how the lawn reacts to each kind.

Fast-release inorganic fertilizers include materials such as ammonium sulfate. They are inexpensive, high-nitrogen fertilizers. Highly soluble in water, they dissolve quickly and don't last long. These fertilizers provide a sudden growth flush that lasts a few weeks, then a rapid slowdown—in other words, feast or famine.

Slow-release fertilizers include natural and synthetic organics. Natural organics are derived from natural materials, such as animal manures, sewage sludge, and grain byproducts. They are long-lasting and safe for plants. Usually, they are low in nitrogen, so it takes quite a bit of product to supply the recommended amount of nutrients. They may be slow to break down and release nitrogen.

Inorganic fast-release sources are salts that pull water from the air; they provide quick growth.

Liquid fertilizers contain fast-release nitrogen, which must be reapplied often.

Slow-release sources are safer to plants. Uniformly sized particles are easy to spread.

Testing soil

Soil tests are the most accurate gauge of a lawn's pH and need for phosphorus and potassium. Test soil every three to five years or when your lawn is not up to snuff.

1 Collect several soil samples randomly around your yard, using a probe. Probes slide into the ground and pull out a core of soil without damaging the lawn. If you don't have one, use a trowel. Take samples 3 inches deep or follow the instructions from the soil test lab.

2 Thoroughly mix the samples, and then measure out 1 cup of soil to send to the testing facility.

Synthetic organic fertilizers are manufactured materials that combine the best of natural and inorganic fertilizers. They are high in nutrients, long-lasting, and safe for plants. They may be fast- or slow-acting. They include materials such as fast-acting urea and slow-acting methylene urea, polymer- or plastic-coated urea, and sulfur-coated urea (also called SCU).

The best lawn fertilizers are a mix of fast and slow materials. The quick-release nitrogen immediately feeds the lawn. It is used up in a few weeks, but by then, nutrients from the slow-release materials are available. In high-quality fertilizers, fast-release materials make up a small portion of the fertilizer. In that way, you're assured of steady, uniform growth.

LIQUID OR DRY?

Fertilizer can be applied to a lawn in liquid or dry form. People often ask which is best. The truth is, lawns don't care. Both contain the same materials and both provide satisfactory results, although liquids are quick-release fertilizers and must be applied more frequently.

The question is more a matter of convenience and skill. It takes more skill to uniformly apply liquid fertilizer at the right rate. Most homeowners generally find dry materials easier to handle, especially if they have a good spreader that accurately and uniformly distributes the fertilizer.

Fertilizer
spreaders

Broadcast spreader
- Good in large areas or when you want to work quickly
- 5- to 10-foot swath, depending on fertilizer and walking speed

Drop spreader
- Very precise
- Good in small areas
- 18- to 24-inch swath
- Use where you want to avoid fertilizing adjacent areas

Handheld crank spreader
- Accuracy depends on how steady you hold your hand and how straight you walk
- 5- to 6-foot swath

Almost everyone knows firsthand the embarrassment of a yellow-striped lawn. You can't hide it from the neighbors, and it takes weeks to go away. After spending time, effort, and money on fertilizing, you may feel it was all a waste.

Striping means that the fertilizer wasn't applied evenly. Usually it results from overlapping too much or too little between passes. It is an extreme sign of misapplication.

The goal when fertilizing is to put the fertilizer down uniformly at the correct rate over the entire lawn. A high-quality spreader can do both; knowing how to operate the spreader ensures that it does.

SELECTING A SPREADER

Most stores offer two basic types of lawn spreaders, drop and broadcast, which you can use to apply many materials besides fertilizer. All have a hopper you pour the fertilizer into, an opening on the bottom of the spreader to release the fertilizer, a way of adjusting the size of the opening to meter the flow from the hopper, and an on-off lever. The two types of spreaders vary in the way they distribute fertilizer, and their distribution pattern is key to which one is appropriate for your yard, as well as how easy it is to avoid striping and make uniform applications.

■ *Drop:* These spreaders apply materials in a well-defined, straight path, with the fertilizer dropping directly down from the hopper. On average, they cover a 2-foot-wide strip, but their wheels extend several inches beyond the drop zone. For that reason, it takes practice to avoid leaving stripes using these spreaders (you need to overlap the wheel tracks).

Drop spreaders are especially suitable when you need to precisely apply fertilizer, such as when spreading around flower and shrub beds, near water gardens, or along pavement. Their narrow width means they take longer to use than does a rotary spreader, but the precision with which they apply fertilizer is key in confined or congested areas.

■ *Broadcast:* Also called rotary spreaders, broadcast spreaders have a spinning disk at the base of the hopper that throws fertilizer in a wide fan-shaped swath in front of the spreader. They're fast but not precise. More fertilizer falls near the hopper than at the edge. Different sizes of particles come out of the hopper at varying rates, and everything within the swath will be fertilized, whether it needs it or not. (Some new models can be adjusted to spread to one side, which keeps materials away from gardens, sidewalks, and driveways.) It's easier to avoid striping the lawn with a rotary spreader; however, you still must overlap for even coverage.

In small yards with many flower beds or water features, use a drop spreader. Select a broadcast spreader for fertilizing large lots. If your large lot has many beds, consider buying one of each type of spreader. Use the drop spreader to make several header strips around the beds, then fill in between them with the broadcast spreader. Or use a broadcast model spreader that can be adjusted to prevent granules from being thrown on landscaping, driveways, and sidewalks.

■ *Handheld crank spreaders:* Hand spreaders are a type of rotary spreader. They are inexpensive and useful in small areas but have some limitations. They hold only a few pounds of fertilizer. They can be even more imprecise than a typical rotary lawn spreader because many people don't have the arm strength to hold a full hopper and steadily turn the cranks without wobbling. Hand spreaders work best in small areas you can cover with just one pass.

Whichever style of spreader you choose, check fertilizer labels before buying. If labels don't specify a setting for the spreader brand you're considering, you'll find it hard to know how much fertilizer to apply. For accurate application and a healthy lawn, purchase a well-known and readily available spreader.

Caring for spreaders

After each use, empty the hopper. Set the opening wide open and thoroughly hose off the spreader—the hopper, the wheels, the spinning rotor, everything. Be sure to get into all nooks and crannies; use a brush on them if you have to, so that no residue is left. Let the spreader dry. Then lightly oil the bottom of the hopper surface, the spring and rod inside the control housing, and the axle bearing.

Finally, store the spreader out of the elements with the hopper wide open.

Tip

Most fertilizer labels specify what setting to use to accurately apply the product at the correct rate. The speed at which you walk will affect the application rate. If you walk much slower than average, you could apply excess fertilizer; walking much faster reduces the amount of fertilizer you put down. Walk at a moderate speed that you can consistently maintain when fertilizing your entire lawn.

Spreading
how-to

If you have a hard time seeing the wheel tracks, fertilize in the early morning when the lawn is still dewy. That's when it's easiest to see where you've been.

Once you get to this point, fertilizing is easy. Fill the hopper and go. A few rules, however, will help you work accurately and evenly.

Push the spreader rather than pull it. Take care to walk a straight line as you push the spreader. Set a steady, moderate pace and maintain it. Speeding up or slowing down changes the rate at which the fertilizer comes out of the spreader.

Know where any sharp dips in the lawn are, such as where the soil has settled after removing a tree. Spreader wheels falling into the depression can spill extra fertilizer there.

Operate the spreader over the "long way" of the lawn. Then you don't stop to turn as often.

In square or rectangular yards with few obstacles, first make two header strips as wide as your spreader's application width at each end of the lawn. Then go back and forth between the headers. Headers give you room to turn. Avoid over-fertilizing the header strip by shutting the hopper just after you reach it.

In an irregularly shaped yard with shrub and flower beds, apply header strips around the beds, then fill in between them. Shut off the hopper when you reach the header strip.

Leave the hopper closed until you start walking. Close the hopper just before coming to a stop. Also close it when turning, when backing, and when reaching a section that you've already applied fertilizer to. If trees or other obstacles get in the way, shut off the spreader just before you reach the trunk. Move to the other side of the tree, open the hopper and start walking.

Keep the fertilizer dry. Dry fertilizer is easier to apply. If you must spread on misty or damp days,

Spills

It's best to fill the spreader on pavement so that any spills are easy to sweep up. However, no matter how careful people are, accidents happen. When they happen on the lawn, take action fast. A spill can kill the grass, and sometimes the effects last for years. Scoop up as much of the spill from the lawn as you can. Using a wet-dry vacuum will help pick up the fine pieces. Then flood the area with water, lots of water. You want the soluble fertilizer to dissolve and move below the root zone, where it won't prevent grass from growing in the future. It may still die but will revive faster.

hopper covers are available to protect the fertilizer. They fit like a shower cap.

Wash the fertilizer off grass blades with ¼ to ½ inch of water, especially if the temperature is above 90°F. Sweep sidewalks and driveways so that fertilizer doesn't end up in storm drains.

AVOID STREAKS AND STRIPES

Overlapping is the key to avoiding stripes. Even so, it's easy to overlap too much or too little and still have streaks, unless you know the tricks.

Rotary spreaders are fairly simple. Make sure you know the width of your spreader's throw pattern, then overlap the edge about a foot. For example, say you know that your spreader applies a 6-foot-wide swath. Shut off the spreader at the header strip. Turn, and walk over 5 feet, then face the lawn again and apply the next swath.

With drop spreaders, you'll need to pay a little more attention. If you have one of the newer models, which has an arrow on top of the hopper, simply align the arrow with the previous swath's wheel track.

Without the arrow, what you want to do is overlap the previous wheel track by an inch or so. An easy way to do that is to pivot the spreader so that the wheel is just inside the previous track. Take care that you overlap just the wheel tracks and not the hopper; the two hopper tracks should just meet. Applying the fertilizer in the early morning when the grass is still dewy can help you see where you've been. Consider practicing on the driveway so you get used to where the fertilizer drops.

If you confuse the spreader tracks with the mower tracks, apply the fertilizer at right angles to the direction you normally mow.

Apply header strips at the ends of the lawn or, when the lawn is irregularly shaped, around the edges. Then fill in between the headers.

Setting up a fertilizer program

You are not on your own when it comes to preparing an annual schedule for your lawn. The better brands of lawn products generally include recommendations of when and how to apply the product as part of the package directions.

Reduce the number of applications by using "fertilizer-plus," or combination products to control a problem while feeding the lawn. Combination products are available to control weeds, insects, or moss. For example, you can buy a lawn fertilizer combined with a crabgrass control or a moss control. These products are formulated to apply the correct amount of the active ingredient to control or prevent a problem, along with the right amount of fertilizer for your lawn.

Use the lists below to develop a program for your lawn. Start the program with the current season rather than waiting for the next year. From that point on, apply the next product at approximately two-month intervals. That's all there is to it. Or sign up for a free email reminder service at www.scotts.com. You supply the zip code to receive timely lawn care advice based on where you live and what type of grass you have. By doing the right thing at the right time, it is easy for everyone to appear to have a green thumb when it comes to improving lawns.

COOL-SEASON GRASSES *(lawns in the Northwest, Northeast, and Midwest)*

- February–April: Fertilize and prevent crabgrass (apply before crabgrass germinates, which is about the same time as dandelion puff balls form). Control moss now if it is a problem.
- April–June: Fertilize and control broadleaf weeds.
- June–August: Fertilize and protect against insects. Moths flying from the grass are a clue that it's time to apply a control product.
- August–September: Fertilize for fall root growth.
- October–November: Winterize, also called fall fertilizing, to prepare the lawn for winter and promote early spring greenup.
- Note: Add grub, moss, or fungus control if you expect problems.

WARM-SEASON GRASSES *(lawns in the South and Southwest)*

- January–March: For most lawns, prevent crabgrass. Fertilize and control weeds for St. Augustinegrass.
- April–June: Fertilize and control broadleaf weeds. (For St. Augustinegrass, use a fertilizer with no weed control.)
- June–August: Fertilize and protect against insects.
- August–September: Fertilize for fall root growth.
- September–October: Winterize— fertilize—prepare your lawn for winter and promote early spring greenup. Do not feed centipedegrass now; limit it to two to three feedings per year.
- Note: Lawns in California and the Southwest can be winterized until mid-December. Also, add grub and fungus control if you expect problems.

Watering

Watering
basics

I n most instances, your goal when watering is to moisten the lawn's entire root zone—from the soil surface to 6 to 8 inches deep—and to keep it moist. That usually takes 1 to 2 inches of water per week, either from rain or irrigation.

Early morning is the best time to water.

This is the ideal. It ensures that roots grow deeply and that they always have a ready water supply. Lawns can get by on much less. In fact, they often survive eight weeks or longer without water. They go dormant and turn brown, but they don't die.

DEEP AND INFREQUENT

The key to meeting the ideal is to water deeply and infrequently. Irrigate once a week, applying the whole amount at once. Or water twice a week, applying at least ½ inch of water at a time.

Watering every day may seem as though your lawn is getting the best of care, but it's not. Frequent watering

Watering daily vs. weekly

Applying ¹⁄₁₀ inch of water daily supplies nearly 1 inch of water a week. Yet the lawn is not as healthy as if you had applied the water in one 1-inch or two ½-inch increments. The more water you apply at one time, the deeper and healthier the root system grows and the more resilient the grass becomes.

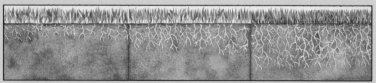

| ¹⁄₁₀ inch per day | ½ inch per week | 1 inch per week |

merely wets the soil surface. The roots proliferate where soil is moist but don't grow any deeper. A shallow-rooted lawn is not able to survive stressful periods.

How long to let your sprinklers run to supply a half inch or more of water depends upon two things: how fast the water comes out of the sprinklers and how fast the soil can absorb it.

Measuring how fast the water comes out is a simple procedure. Set a few straight-sided containers around your lawn (12-ounce soup cans are best; water splashes out of shallow cans). Note the time, turn the sprinklers on, and leave them on for 20 minutes, or until water begins to run off. Measure the depth of the water in all the cans.

If the least-filled can holds ¼ inch of water, your sprinklers will take 80 minutes to deliver an inch of water to all parts of the lawn. Here's how you figure the time: Divide 1 inch by the amount in the can (1 ÷ ¼ = 4). Then multiply the result by 20 minutes (4 × 20 = 80 minutes).

Soil can't always soak up the water as fast as the sprinkler supplies it. If water runs into the street after 10 minutes, that's as long as you can operate the sprinklers at one time. In that case, if the least-filled can is ¼ inch deep, it will take 40 minutes to apply an inch of water (4 × 10). To ensure it all soaks into the lawn, run the sprinklers in four 10-minute cycles with 20 to 30 minutes—or however long it takes for the water to soak in—between each cycle.

How the grasses rank

NEEDS THE MOST WATER
- ■ Bentgrass
- ■ Perennial ryegrass
- ■ Kentucky bluegrass
- ■ Fescues
- ■ St. Augustinegrass
- ■ Bahiagrass
- ☐ Centipedegrass
- ☐ Zoysiagrass
- ☐ Bermudagrass
- ☐ Buffalograss

NEEDS THE LEAST WATER

WHEN TO WATER

Early morning is the most efficient time to water. Municipal water pressure is at its peak, and there's usually less wind to distort the spray from its intended target. Also the lawn has all day to dry before nightfall. Wet foliage overnight promotes diseases.

You can make an exception to this rule in the Southwest and areas with very low humidity and high daytime temperatures. In those areas, less water is lost to evaporation if you water at night.

It's impossible to define a watering schedule that applies to every situation. Keeping the root zone moist may mean watering every three or four days, or every 10 to 15 days. Exactly how often and how much you should water depends upon many factors, primarily the type of soil, the weather, and the type of grass. Learn the variables of your yard and climate; then you'll know how to apply the water-deeply-and-infrequently rule to your lawn.

Sprinklers & irrigation systems

I f you live where lawns occasionally need supplemental watering— or depend upon it for much of the year—you'll need a watering system. You have two choices: portable or permanent. Water reaches portable sprinklers through hoses; permanent irrigation systems, through buried pipes.

Simplest and cheapest is a portable sprinkler-and-hose arrangement—the way to go if you rarely need to water. But if you water every week, an in-ground, permanent sprinkler system saves effort over the long haul. More expensive initially, an in-ground system is much more convenient and efficient.

There are advantages and disadvantages to both systems. Buy the best quality you can afford, buy what best matches your lot, and use it right.

PORTABLE SPRINKLERS

Portable sprinklers are usually inexpensive; they are certainly flexible, especially compared to a permanent system. To water a large lawn, they have to be moved around by hand.

Impact sprinklers have the most uniform distribution pattern and efficiently cover large areas.

Some portable sprinklers have a built-in timer or gauge. Some allow you to set the sprinkler to run for a certain number of minutes, others, for a number of gallons. Both are useful if you know how to use the information.

It is important that you test whatever kind of sprinkler you use. Do the soup-can test described on page 17 to see how many minutes it takes to apply a specific amount of water and where any gaps in coverage occur. That's the only way you'll know how long to let the sprinkler run and where to place and move it so that the entire lawn is watered. Following are five popular types of sprinklers.

Garden hoses

Buy the best hose you can. Inexpensive hoses are often too skinny to deliver enough water and too stiff to handle. As a result, you may avoid using them, and the lawn suffers.

Hoses come in three diameters. Most are ⅝ inch; ½-inch hoses are too small; ¾-inch hoses deliver more water but are heavy and more expensive.

Garden hoses are rated by their number of reinforcing layers, or plies. Three-ply hoses are the lightest duty. Best for long-term service are four- or five-ply hoses.

Common materials are vinyl and rubber. Vinyl is cheaper and lighter; rubber is more expensive, less prone to kinking, and heavier. The best option is a combination of both materials.

■ **Stationary sprinklers** are the most basic of sprinklers—not much more complicated than putting your finger over the end of a hose. Best use: Small areas that other sprinklers miss or that need supplemental water.

■ **Impact and rotary sprinklers** rotate through the combined action of a spring-loaded counterweight bouncing off the water stream. These sprinklers always water a circular area, but you can adjust a set of tabs or stops to control how much of the circle they cover, between 15 and 360 degrees. Best use: Medium to large lawns that can accommodate a circular pattern.

■ **Oscillating sprinklers** move a fan of water over large, rectangular areas. The sprinkler shoots thin streams high into the air while a geared mechanism powered by the water stream moves the fan back and forth. Because the water streams are thin, even a light gust of wind can blow them off course. Best use: Whenever you need a low delivery rate, whether for a new seedbed or where runoff is a problem.

Traveling sprinklers have fairly uniform distribution. Take care when laying out their path to ensure all areas are covered.

■ **Revolving sprinklers** shoot jets of water in a circular pattern from one or more rotating arms. Best use: For watering small areas where runoff is not a problem.

■ **Traveling sprinklers** move by themselves. They spray like revolving sprinklers with spinning arms, but while doing so, they also travel along a track of hose. Best use: Large and level lawns.

PERMANENT SPRINKLERS

Think of a permanent irrigation system as an insurance policy that protects your investment in your lawn. The greater the value your lawn has for you, the more reasonable it is to invest in a high-quality sprinkler system.

Many types of spray heads are available for in-ground irrigation systems, allowing you to match the rate of application to the variables of your lawn.

In-ground systems are not for everyone. A permanent system makes watering lawns more convenient and efficient, but if you water only occasionally, it's not worth the expense. A major concern is cost. Although prices vary widely according to the size of the property and its particular needs, a typical system can cost $1,500 to $2,000. A significant sum to be sure, but the sprinkler system will pay for itself if it results in a healthier, more drought-resistant lawn.

The best time to install an underground system is just before planting the seed or sod but after the soil is level and graded. Digging trenches is relatively easy at that time. Plus, if you wait until the grass is in place, you'll damage the lawn.

Conserving
water

Mowing high helps conserve water. The grass more efficiently uses the water that's available.

Water conservation is an important issue. Mandated watering restrictions are a fact of life in many regions, especially those with cyclical droughts. No matter where you live, it's best to plan ahead.

If water restrictions are declared, don't panic. Although the lawn won't stay green, grass has an incredible ability to survive extended droughts. This is particularly true of the grasses that spread by underground rhizomes, such as bermudagrass, zoysiagrass, and Kentucky bluegrass. Rhizomes have buds that, once moisture is restored—even after months of drought—will begin to grow. Lawns that appear dead can be restored to a healthy, dense condition in just a few weeks.

A healthy, vigorous, well-managed lawn will endure and recover best from extended drought. A deep root system is vital during drought. Established roots will mine for water and shrug off dry conditions. The key to ensuring your lawn will return after a drought is taking care of the lawn before the drought starts. Then you'll be more likely to have a lawn once the dry period ends.

■ *Fertility:* Lawns that are starved for nutrients may have a smaller root system and are not as efficient at obtaining water from the soil. This can easily be observed during dry periods when unirrigated lawns begin to go into dormancy. Fertilized lawns will remain green for several days, or even weeks, longer than lawns that are not fed on a regular basis.

■ *Mowing height:* Mow at the tallest cutting height recommended for the grass species in your lawn (see page 26). No matter the type of grass, the higher you mow, the deeper the roots and the more water-efficient the lawn. That's because a plant with an extensive root system is better able to tap into available soil moisture than is a plant with a shallow, restricted root system.

■ *Watering:* Adapt the lawn to deep, infrequent irrigation before a drought begins. A lawn used to overwatering or frequent light irrigation will suffer the most because of its shallow root system.

During a drought, it's often better to restrict all water to the lawn than provide a little. The small amount of water might prevent the desirable grass from entering dormancy, but it will certainly encourage weeds.

■ *Aerate:* Core aeration opens the thatch layer and improves water infiltration into the root zone. The timing of this task is important. Spring is the best time for warm-season grasses. Aerate cool-season lawns in late summer or early fall.

Timers for sprinklers

Various types of timers are available that can make watering your lawn more convenient and perhaps more efficient. The simplest kinds connect faucet to hose and shut off the sprinkler after either a set amount of time has passed or a number of gallons of water has been applied. These timers cost less than $15. Although their capacity and adaptability are limited, they work well, assuring that the sprinkler will not be left on all night. Some sprinklers have timers integrated into their design.

Battery-powered timers (costing $30–$40) connect just as simply but turn sprinklers both on and off and provide up to four watering cycles a day. They are a big help when you must cycle water on and off to prevent runoff.

Conserving water
continued

WHERE DROUGHT IS THE NORM

Think about replanting your lawn with a native grass. Even considering the energy and expense starting a lawn from scratch requires, it makes sense to grow a species that is adapted to the climate and availability of water in your area. For example, buffalograss, a native of the short-grass prairie in the United States, is a good choice for mild, dry areas from Montana to Mexico.

Take the time to find the most appropriate species for your region. Also, be sure to learn about the grass's maintenance requirements. Not all native grasses do well with the same care you give typical lawn grasses.

Many native grasses, such as buffalograss, do well in dry areas. They're usually less suited to "manicuring."

If a native species isn't an option, consider switching your lawn to a more drought-tolerant species, such as tall fescue in cool areas or bermudagrass in warm ones. To learn more, contact your local extension service and inquire about drought-tolerant grasses for your area.

Mowing

Mowing
basics

There are really only two rules to mowing: Remove no more than one-third of the grass blade at one time and mow at the upper range of the recommended cutting height for your grass.

Growing heights vary for each grass species, but the taller you keep the grass, the stronger it will be and the better able to survive periods of stress. This is especially important during the summer, when the taller height also prevents germination of weed seeds and insulates the soil during periods of drought.

HINTS FOR SMOOTH MOWING:
1. Mow header strips at the ends of the lawn and around flower beds and shrub borders.

A CHANGE IN TRADITION

Turf specialists used to recommend cutting the grass shorter than normal the first time you mow in spring. This low cutting was believed to allow the sun to reach into the crowns of the grass plants and stimulate new growth for early greenup. Experts now say this early scalping may do more harm than good. In fact, scalping at any time of year can severely damage your lawn—especially during times of stress, such as extended hot, dry periods for cool-season grasses.

2. Mow back and forth between the header strips. The headers allow room to turn and work around curves.

That's because scalping—cutting off more than a third of the leaf—forces the plant to put its energy into regrowing blades instead of roots. It also exposes the lower, shaded parts of the plant to sunlight, turning them into an unsightly gray-brown stubble. So even though it may not look as trim and tidy, taller grass is stronger and healthier grass.

To avoid scalping, mow often enough that you never remove more than one third of the grass blade. The recommended height for Kentucky bluegrass is about 2 inches, which means you should mow as soon as it reaches 3 inches tall. Similarly, tall fescue thrives at $3\frac{1}{2}$ inches; mow it when it is $4\frac{1}{2}$ to 5 inches tall.

How do you measure height? Mower decks generally have a range of $\frac{5}{8}$ inch to $3\frac{1}{2}$ inches. To check height, place the mower on a hard surface, disconnect the spark plug, and measure the distance between the blades and the hard surface with a tape measure (or use a stiff piece of paper and pencil).

Keeping in mind the basic concept of mowing high and often, turn the page for specific recommendations for mowing cool- and warm-season grasses.

3. Overlap each cut by 1 or 2 inches to avoid giving your lawn a Mohawk haircut with each pass.

Mowing tips

■ Be sure your mower blade is sharp. Sharp blades cut the grass cleanly and help mulch clippings into small pieces, which break down quickly. Conversely, dull mower blades shred the grass, leaving a ragged cut at the top of the blade, which gives the lawn a whitish, diseased appearance. Some grasses, such as perennial ryegrass, take on a particularly ragged look if mowed with a dull blade. Keep a spare sharp blade handy to quickly replace a dull one.

■ Change the direction and pattern each time you mow. Doing so reduces turf wear from mower wheels. This damage is even more pronounced in thin or shady areas. If you mow repeatedly in the same direction, the mower tends to push the grass over rather than cut it cleanly. Eventually, the grass begins to lean in the direction mowed, producing light and dark patterns or stripes.

■ Don't allow newly seeded grass to grow excessively long before the first mowing. If the grass gets too tall before mowing and you mow it to, say, half its height, you'll shock the plants, stressing them and slowing the process of forming a healthy lawn.

Mowing basics

continued

COOL-SEASON GRASSES

You can set the mower as high as it will go and never touch the setting again with cool-season grasses (bluegrass, ryegrass, and fescue). But if you want athletic-field and golf-course quality, start the season by mowing at the low end of the height range. Raise the setting to the tallest recommended height in summer. Hot weather stresses the grass, and the additional foliage provides shade that lowers soil temperature and slows water loss during hot weather. Longer blades also provide greater surface area, allowing the plant to manufacture more carbohydrates to feed the roots. Mow frequently because too-tall grass can become coarse, stemmy, and matted.

Cool-season grasses grow vigorously during the spring and will require more frequent cutting then. Continue mowing until the grass stops growing in fall, when the weather turns cooler and the foliage starts to change color.

WARM-SEASON GRASSES

Warm-season grasses (bermudagrass, St. Augustinegrass, and zoysiagrass) are better adapted to warm weather than cool-season grasses. You don't need to raise the mower height to protect them from heat stress. But bermudagrass and zoysiagrass do build up excessive thatch if maintained at levels higher than 1½ and 2½ inches, respectively.

Some warm-season grass species can survive mowing heights as low as ⅛ inch, while others won't do well below 1½ inches. Warm-season grasses thrive at such low heights because of the presence of stolons; they spread by sending out lateral stems along the ground, making it possible for them to grow under conditions that kill more upright grasses. So keep the cutting height the same all summer for these grasses because they aren't affected by heat and they experience more vigorous growth during the summer.

Recommended mowing heights

In general, mow your lawn on the highest blade setting possible. Follow the rule of thirds when it comes to frequency—only remove one-third of the grass blade at a time when mowing. Bermudagrass and zoysiagrass are exceptions. They are best maintained at a height of 2 inches.

Squiggles and checks

Heard the latest in lawn fashion? Inspired by the grounds at baseball parks, many homeowners are embellishing lawns with checkerboards, stripes, plaids, diamonds, and squiggles. The designs result from light reflecting off the grass. Try it for yourself. Push the grass away from you, and it has a bright, reflective surface; pull the blades toward you, and the surface is dark. Expressive groundskeeping is easy with the right equipment. Professionals use a mower with a weighted roller that pushes down the grass blades to highlight the pattern. Residential models and roller attachments are available. To make a checkerboard, mow back and forth, alternating directions with each pass. Next, go over the lawn at right angles to the first mowing. Finish by going over every other stripe from the first mowing, all in the same direction.

FIGURE THE FREQUENCY

How often should you cut the grass? The simple answer is, as often as it takes to maintain its recommended height. That depends on the species of grass, the season, growing conditions, and the amount and type of fertilizer used. Generally, every five to seven days is enough, keeping the basic rule of thirds in mind. It's also important to cut the grass regularly throughout the growing season. The more moisture the grass receives, the more often you'll need to cut it. You may find yourself mowing twice a week during extended periods of rain. During wet periods some specialists suggest a practice known as double cutting. This involves moving the mower height up a setting during wet periods, then, after the clippings dry, lowering the mower to the correct height and mowing a second time in a different direction. Similarly, a dry spell might provide a mowing break. Resist the urge to mow too low during dry periods. Low mowing further stresses the grass.

Lawn mowers

WALK-BEHIND
Walk-behind mowers offer an unlimited range of options, from width of cut to horsepower, matching any situation.

The two most common types of lawn mowers are rotary and reel. Reel mowers are lightweight, inexpensive, and powered by good old muscle power. If your lawn is less than 2,000 square feet consider a reel mower.

Most mowers on the market are gas-powered rotary models, with 2- or 4-cycle engines. Rotaries employ a single blade that is mounted horizontally and spins at speeds up to 200 miles per hour.

You can select from an array of features and models among the many rotary mowers available. If you want to avoid exertion and your pockets are deep enough, there are new, high-tech robotic models.

ROTARY MOWERS

The rotary mower is by far the most common type used on lawns in the United States and Canada. You'll find electric, gas, and battery-powered models. A rotary mower blade is easy to remove, and anyone with a grinding stone or file can sharpen one with practice. Or you can take the blade to a shop for sharpening.

Rotary mowers are much safer than they were even a few years ago. Two types of safety systems are available. The most common is what is known as a zone restart, a lever or switch that stops both the blade and the engine. More expensive models feature a blade-brake clutch (or dead-man's switch), a safety bar on the handle that stops only the blade from spinning, not the engine, as soon as it's released. Don't defeat the safety devices. The spinning blade can sever fingers, toes, hands, and feet.

Safety

■ **Understand how the equipment works.** Read the owner's manual before starting or using equipment for the first time. Know where all the controls are located.

■ **Dress to mow.** Wear long pants and close-fitting clothes, and always wear sturdy shoes.

■ **Clear the area.** Pick up rocks, twigs, golf balls, and anything else the mower could throw.

■ **Handle gas carefully.** Fill the tank before starting, while the engine is cool. Avoid spills. Store gasoline in an approved container in a cool, well-ventilated area. Never smoke around a mower. When you're ready to start the mower, do so outdoors.

■ **Keep children and pets away** from the mower. Never allow kids to play with a mower or operate it without supervision. Don't carry a child with you on a riding mower. Many children have fallen off and been cut by the blades before the engine could be stopped.

■ **Never pull a mower toward you.** If you should slip, you could catch a foot under the mower blade.

Rotary mowers—which come in side-discharge, rear-discharge, bagging, and mulching models—are best suited to taller mowing heights and are more likely to scalp bumpy or uneven lawns at levels lower than 1 inch.

Don't skimp on engine capability. The engines on lower-priced models tend to have power ratings between 2.5 and 3.0 horsepower. Tall, dense grass can bend their crankshafts. A mower with an engine capability of 3.5 or higher is better for such lawns.

If you intend to leave clippings on the lawn, mulching mowers will do a good job of slicing and dicing them into small pieces so they'll disappear quickly. The key to getting clippings to break down rapidly, though, is to mow often enough that the clippings are never so thick they smother the grass beneath them.

SELECT A POWER SOURCE

■ **Gas-powered mowers:** If your yard is up to a half acre in size, you'll probably want a gas-powered, walk-behind model, although the engine makes for a heavy mower (up to 100 pounds) that's less easy to handle than an electric model. Even so, gas mowers have been the most popular sellers for many years. They simply have more power and work better for large lawns. Self-propelled versions take the work out of slopes and thick turf.

■ **Electric mowers:** Electric push mowers don't pollute the air and are quiet, easy to maintain, and relatively inexpensive. You'll find electric push models powered by either an electric cord or a battery. Corded machines are good for small lawns where maneuverability isn't a problem. The main disadvantage of electric mowers is that you have to drag around an extension cord.

■ **Battery-powered mowers:** These mowers are much easier to maneuver around a yard—and a bit more expensive—than their tethered cousins. You'll find them heavier (55 to 80 pounds), so you might wish to buy a self-propelled model, especially if your lawn slopes.

Most battery-powered mowers can cut up to 5,000 square feet on a single charge—about 45 minutes of mowing time.

■ **Riding mowers:** The next step up is a riding mower—more expensive and more powerful than any of the walk-behind varieties. A riding mower makes the most sense for homeowners with truly large lawns or physical conditions that limit activity. The typical 30- to 42-inch mowing path is a major plus for big jobs.

Consider buying a garden tractor if you have several acres or more to maintain. These machines can cut the grass and also till soil, scoop snow, and pull large loads. Take care when using both types of riders on steep slopes.

ZERO-TURNING RADIUS

The rear wheels of zero-turn mowers operate independently, giving you the ability to cut closer to objects, turn tighter corners, and reduce the trimming that follows later. These popular mowers are fun to drive but take some getting used to. Consider buying one if your lot is large or you have little time to mow.

Lawn mower
maintenance

MAINTAINING YOUR INVESTMENT

You've spent a lot of money on your lawn mower, and you want the machine to last. The best way to assure that is to set up—and follow—a comprehensive maintenance schedule. Your owner's manual is a good place to start your to-do list. If you bought a used lawn mower or don't have the owner's manual, check the suggestions on page 31, *opposite*.

■ *Spring prep:* Read the manual. Most manuals tell you what you need to know. Pay close attention to the viscosity and quality of oil recommended for the engine. The wrong oil can cause overheating and excessive wear on the internal parts.

Keep the air filter clean. A dirty filter causes the engine to work harder and waste energy. It also permits particles to enter the internal workings of the mower, wearing them down and causing pitting. The mower will begin burning oil, like a worn-out car engine.

Inspect or change the spark plug either at the beginning or end of each mowing season. Use a spark-plug gauge to check the gap; most manuals list the gap thickness. Take care not to damage the porcelain insulator. If the porcelain is cracked, replace the plug; it won't be able to transfer heat from the engine.

■ *Winter storage:* At the end of the mowing season, put the machine away for the winter. Allow the engine to cool completely. Drain most of the gas from the fuel tank, then run the mower until the entire fuel system is completely dry. Or add a fuel stabilizer to the tank. (First, consult the owner's manual; using an additive may void the warranty.)

Drain and properly dispose of the old crankcase oil and replace it with fresh oil per owner's manual instructions.

Remove the spark plug, using a spark-plug wrench. Lubricate the cylinder by pouring a teaspoon of oil through the spark-plug hole (again, check the instructions in your owner's manual). Slowly rotate the engine several times by turning the crankshaft or pulling the starter rope to distribute the oil. Replace the spark plug with a new one, but don't reconnect the spark-plug wire to it.

Thoroughly clean all dirt and debris from the machine. If you have a self-propelled mower, grease the rear height-adjuster brackets. Check the blade and engine-mounting bolts to make sure all are tight. This is also a good time to inspect and sharpen the blade.

Store the mower in a dry place, away from appliances with pilot lights or other potential ignition sources.

Maintenance steps

BEGINNING OF SEASON

- Add fresh gas
- Replace spark plug
- Sharpen blade
- Clean or replace air filter
- Check oil level
- Inflate riding mower tires
- Reconnect spark-plug wire

PERIODICALLY

- Clean or change air filter after every 25 hours—more often if working in dusty conditions
- Lubricate wheels and moving joints after 25 hours
- Check belts and chain drives of riding mowers

END OF SEASON

- Change oil
- Drain gas or add gas stabilizer
- Lubricate cylinder
- Thoroughly clean mower
- Grease where necessary
- Store safely
- Disconnect spark-plug wire

BEFORE EACH USE

- Check fuel and oil levels
- Check tire inflation
- Check for loose or worn parts
- Reconnect spark-plug wire

AFTER EACH USE

- Clean clippings from underside of mower and from top of deck

THROUGHOUT THE SEASON

- Check blade sharpness and general condition
- Balance the blade after sharpening
- Check all visible moving parts for wear and looseness
- Use correct fuel and oil

Finishing touches

The edges of a lawn where grass meets planting beds or paved areas have a big impact. Letting them grow shaggy gives the whole lawn a messy, unkempt appearance. It takes little effort to keep edges looking orderly.

String trimmers and power edgers help you attain that well-manicured appearance you desire and make the job easier.

MAINTAINING AN EDGE

String trimmers may be powered either by a gasoline engine or an electric motor. Gas models are the most powerful and versatile. Always wear eye protection when using a string trimmer. The spinning nylon string can throw small objects at a high rate of speed and damage eyes. Long pants take the sting out of the job too.

As a lawn grows, it builds up organic matter and collects windblown soil at its edges. The resulting buildup lets grass grow a few inches over sidewalks, driveways, and street curbs. You can easily remove it with an edger—a tool designed to cut a neat line between pavement and lawn. Manual or power edgers are available.

Power and roller edgers are easiest to use on long, straight edges. Half-moon edgers and string trimmers are good for cleaning up around the irregular edges of shrub and flower beds.

Straight-shaft trimmers are powerful and comfortable to use. Try out a trimmer before buying to ensure that its length and weight fit your body.

Protecting tree trunks

Never use a string trimmer to trim grass near a tree trunk (or bang your mower against the bark). That little bit of damage can kill the tree, especially if you do it every week. It destroys the tree's water- and food-conducting tissue and provides an entrance for insects and diseases.

A good way to protect the tree is to install a ring of mulch around the trunk. Make the ring as wide as the drip line of the tree (the outside edge of the canopy). This protects the trunk from nicks and cuts and makes the tree healthier because grass inhibits tree-root growth.

Another alternative is to plant groundcover around the tree.

Managing
thatch and
compaction

Thatch
basics

A little thatch, up to ½ inch, is good. Any thicker than that, and you will need to take action to maintain the quality of your lawn.

Excess thatch—a layer of dead organic matter and living plant parts—is a common problem. Just as people slough dead skin cells and pets shed fur, so do grass plants cast off their dead tissues. Organisms in the soil—microbes, earthworms, and insects—feed on the dead matter and break it down. Thatch develops when organic matter accumulates faster than the organisms can deal with it.

That happens when you overfertilize and water frequently and shallowly. With an excess of nitrogen, the grass grows too fast for the organisms. Excess water drives oxygen, which the organisms need for survival, out of the soil. Very high or very low soil pH may also negatively impact the organisms and, thus, lead to thatch.

In thatchy lawns, the grass crown rides on top of the thatch, rather than under it, where it's insulated from heat and cold. Roots may grow into the thatch but not the soil, so the lawn is more susceptible to drought. The lawn also needs more fertilizer because thatch isn't a good source of nutrients. Thatch harbors pathogens and insect pests, and it impedes water infiltration.

How do you determine whether your lawn is excessively thatchy? Thatchy lawns tend to be puffy, or uneven, and easy to scalp as you mow. Look for dry and dead patches of grass and an unusual sponginess or springiness when you walk on it. (Imagine what it would feel like to walk on a sponge.)

Remove a pie-shaped plug of grass with a knife or trowel, or remove a core with a soil probe. Dig deep enough to get some of the soil below. Carefully examine the plug so that you can identify the soil, the grass, and the spongy thatch layer in between. Then measure the depth of the thatch. One-half inch of thatch or less is not a problem. If there is more than that, your lawn is ready for a thatch-management program.

Thatch-prone grasses

Zoysiagrass and St. Augustinegrass are thatch-prone species. They are also easily damaged by dethatching. For maximum recovery, dethatch these grasses in the spring when they begin growing. The lawn will look rough for a couple of weeks as it recovers.

CONTROLLING THATCH

Prevention is key. Most lawns may never have a thatch problem if you follow an annual fertilizer program, water properly, and apply lime or sulfur if a soil test indicates the pH is too high or too low.

You can mechanically eliminate thatch by dethatching. If thatch is a problem, you may need to dethatch once a year until it is corrected. It is very important to follow an annual fertilizer program, water properly, and monitor pH in order stop excessive thatch production and maintain a healthy lawn. Otherwise, you will have to constantly have to dethatch your lawn.

Tips for preventing thatch

- Minimize activities that compact soil
- Mow frequently—before the grass becomes excessively tall
- Follow an annual fertilizer program that is appropriate for your region, and don't exceed recommended rates
- Resist planting vigorously growing grasses and those that produce large amounts of tough, fibrous tissue
- Don't let soil pH fall below 6.0
- Avoid frequent, shallow irrigation

Dethatching

Dethatching involves cutting through the thatch layer and raking out the debris. You can use a special dethatching cavex rake. It has sharp knifelike blades instead of tines and is best for small lawns and people who enjoy hard, physical work. More practical are gas-powered vertical mowers and power rakes. These are essentially the same machine with a choice of different, rapidly spinning vertical reels. Blades on vertical mower reels are solidly attached; those on power rakes swing loosely. The blades of power rakes give when they hit rocks and debris in the lawn, so the machine is less likely to suffer damage. Rent a power rake or vertical mower at your local rental center.

A word of caution: Power raking and vertical mowing can damage centipedegrass, St. Augustinegrass, and others that spread by means of surface runners. Take care when dethatching them. Use a machine that has the knives correctly spaced for these grasses.

Time to dethatch

Dethatch when the grass will most readily recover from the damage, but avoid the primary germination period of the main weeds in your region. The red asterisks on the graphs below mark the best time to dethatch warm- and cool-season grasses.

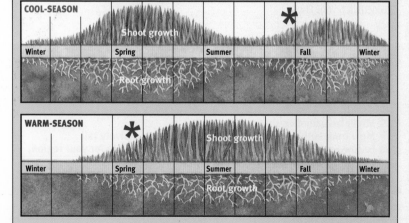

COOL-SEASON
Shoot growth
*
Winter | Spring | Summer | Fall | Winter
Root growth

WARM-SEASON
*
Shoot growth
Winter | Spring | Summer | Fall | Winter
Root growth

TIMING

When to dethatch depends on the type of grass in your lawn. The ideal time for cool-season lawns is late summer or early fall. Then, the grass readily recovers and doesn't have to compete with weeds because few germinate at this time. Dethatch at least 30 days prior to the end of the growing season, before the ground freezes, so the grass has time to recover. You can also dethatch cool-season grasses in the spring, before they start to green up, but because of weed invasion, it's not the best time.

For warm-season lawns, late spring is the best time. Schedule dethatching after the turf greens up but before the hot, dry summer months set in. A good general rule is to dethatch after the second mowing. Follow with a preemergence weed control to discourage crabgrass from germinating.

The power unit is the same for vertical mowers and power rakes. The only difference is the reel. If you want to vertical mow, you attach the stationary reel (*left*). To power rake, attach the flexible reel (*right*).

STEP-BY-STEP

For best results, dethatch after a light rain or water the lawn beforehand. Avoid dethatching when the soil is saturated because the equipment will tear and pull the soil instead of slicing and lifting out the thatch.

Prepare your lawn for dethatching by mowing at the lowest recommended height for your grass. Remove the clippings. If using power equipment, locate and mark all sprinkler heads, shallow irrigation pipes, and cable and phone lines that might be near the soil surface. Then dethatch.

The power rakes and vertical mowers available to homeowners are generally lightweight and low-powered. You will need to make several passes to bring up the thatch. Make subsequent passes

perpendicular to the previous one. Don't attempt to remove the entire layer in one day; multiple passes may damage the lawn and the raking action tends to dry the soil, which can thin the lawn. Be aware that it's possible to pull up enough thatch to fill several garbage bags from a small but heavily thatched lawn.

After you've finished raking, fertilize and then irrigate. This prevents excessive drying out and helps the grass recover from injury.

Use a cavex rake to dethatch small areas by hand. The tines are actually sharp blades and are more effective than a garden rake.

Compaction and aerating

Aerating—also called coring or aerifying—is the best way to improve compacted lawns. Excessive foot or vehicle traffic press soil particles together, preventing necessary oxygen and water from reaching grass roots. Aerating punches holes in the soil, creating a conduit for water and oxygen to flow directly down to the grass roots. In turn, microorganisms thrive and create an excellent growing environment for the grass. The holes eventually refill themselves but the permeability of the soil remains vastly improved.

Use a core aerator that punches holes in the ground and removes small, fingerlike cores, or plugs, of grass and soil. Or hire a professional lawn care company to do the job.

EQUIPMENT

In general, tines on core aerators make 2- to 3-inch-deep holes that are 2 to 4 inches apart. Some aerators have drum-mounted tines that dig into the soil; others have vertical tines that move up and down at a high rate of speed. Still others use solid tines or blades to poke holes without removing cores or to slice the soil. These are less effective than the ones that remove cores. The cores create a topdressing as they crumble, further enhancing thatch breakdown. Rent a core aerator at a local rental center.

Make one pass with the aerator; then make a second pass at a right angle to the first.

TIMING

Coring can have drawbacks. It is hard on plants if you aerate when they are not actively growing. And bringing soil containing weed seeds to the surface encourages weeds such as crabgrass to grow. Timing will help eliminate these problems.

Like dethatching, aerate during the grass's peak growth period. That's late summer or early fall for cool-season grasses and spring for warm-season species—both seasons if the lawn has a severe problem. It's best to not aerate any type of grass during high-temperature stress periods. Plan the fall project early enough to give your lawn the opportunity to recover before winter dormancy, at least 30 days before the ground freezes.

Avoid the primary germination period of the main weeds in your area (crabgrass, goosegrass, and other summer annual weeds germinate in spring). Applying a preemergence herbicide after aerating will help keep them in check.

HOW-TO

Lightly water the lawn the day before you aerate so the tines readily enter the soil and the plugs come out easily. (Don't overwater, though. You'll create a muddy mess, which will be more likely to form a hardpan.) Be sure to flag all sprinkler heads and shallow pipes and wires.

Make two passes. The second pass should be at a right angle to the first to ensure even spacing between holes. Let the cores dry, then use a garden rake or drag a section of chainlink fencing across the lawn to break up the cores and work some of the material back into the holes. Any remaining material will disintegrate after mowing.

For small jobs, up to 1,000 square feet, consider using a handheld corer. These tools perform the same function of the powered units at a fraction of the cost. As when using a cavex rake, plan on getting some hard exercise doing the job. Plunge the tines into the ground, rock the corer back and forth, and pull out the tines.

Slowing compaction

■ Reduce the negative effects of foot traffic by creating walkways in areas that receive constant use
■ Avoid driving heavy vehicles on lawn
■ Establish designated play areas, including access paths to them
■ Mow as often as necessary to follow the rule of thirds

Root growth

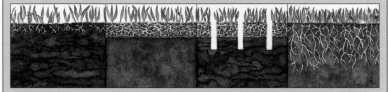

Dense, compacted soil (*far left*) and thick layers of thatch (*center left*) restrict rooting and, in turn, impair the health of the lawn. Compacted soil has no pore space for oxygen, moisture, or roots to move through; thatch forms a physical barrier. Aerating (*center right*) eases both conditions by creating openings in the soil, allowing air and water to enter. Microbes begin to flourish and break down the thatch. Roots again proliferate (*far right*), growing thickly and deeply.

Myths, facts, and advice about thatch

■ **Myth:** All thatch is bad.

■ **Fact:** A thin layer of thatch, ½ inch or less, is natural and beneficial, like a layer of mulch in a garden.

■ **Advice:** Don't worry about a thin layer. Dethatch or aerate only when the thatch is thicker than ½ inch.

■ **Myth:** Leaving clippings on the lawn causes thatch.

■ **Fact:** Clippings do not add to thatch. They are mostly water and contain nutrients. Thatch is composed of stems and crowns.

■ **Advice:** Mow often, never removing more than one-third of the grass height at once, and leave the clippings on the lawn.

■ **Myth:** Compaction alone can not kill grass.

Less than ½-inch layer of thatch

More than ½-inch layer of thatch

■ **Fact:** Compaction can be a severe problem and can kill grass. Large trucks and repeat passes by small cars will create excessive compaction. Truck traffic is especially problematic around home improvement projects where large vehicles drive across an established lawn.

■ **Myth:** Wearing golf or other spiked shoes while mowing eliminates thatch as effectively as aerating does.

■ **Fact:** Spiked shoes will improve your traction while mowing, but the spikes are too shallow and too narrow to eliminate thatch.

Troubleshooting

Identifying
the problem

Lawn problems are solved in four steps: identifying the culprit, stopping its damage, changing an environmental or cultural weak spot that allows the problem to occur, and repairing the damage.

IDENTIFYING LAWN PESTS

Just as doctors use several methods to diagnose an illness, you need to use all the faculties at your disposal to identify lawn problems. Besides using the tools and information you find in this chapter, also talk to your neighbors, to garden center staff, and to local extension service personnel. You will also find help at the Scotts website— www.scotts.com—which has more than 1,500 pages of information, along with an e-mail link to lawn experts. You can also phone Scotts at 800-543-TURF (8873).

As you diagnose your lawn's ailments, it will help to have in mind how you currently take care of your lawn and how that compares with ideal care. This will help you decide whether the problem arises from an environmental or cultural factor. Study Chapters 2 through 4; those chapters point out some of the problems that develop when care is not ideal.

Being a lawn detective means checking the grass from the tip of its blades to its roots to ferret out all symptoms and signs.

WHAT ARE LAWN PESTS?

Lawns support a host of creatures, from microscopic fungi to browsing rabbits and meadow mice. The grass has defenses against many creatures, but mounting the defense takes energy. Strong, vigorous grass plants are the ones best able to fight off pests.

■ *Weeds:* Weeds do not prey on the grass directly as other pests do, but compete with the grass for sunlight, food, and water. Again, the grass can hold its own if it's strong and vigorous, but it can't put up a good battle if it's growing slowly because of a lack or excess of food, water, and general care.

Most weeds are pioneers. They regularly explore new territory for suitable habitat. Many are adapted to different environments than well-maintained lawns. For that reason, they can take advantage of a lawn that is too dry or too wet; shaded or underfed; physically damaged by traffic, insects, and other pests; or mowed incorrectly.

■ *Insect pests:* The variety among insects is astounding. Most are not pests. Those that are can attack from many directions: the soil, the leaves, even from inside the plant.

■ *Pathogens:* Pathogens are disease-causing organisms. Most of them are fungi; a few are other types of microorganisms. Most invade grass blades or roots and grow within the cells, causing disease symptoms.

■ **Animal pests:** Because of their size, animals can do a considerable amount of damage. One mole or gopher can make a mess of a lawn in just a matter of days. Most are not direct pests of the lawn. They usually tear it up looking for insects and earthworms to eat.

■ **Cultural and environmental problems:** This is a catchall that includes all problems not caused by some living creature. For example, the brown spots in a lawn could easily be from a disease or insect or they could be from drought damage, salts put down to melt ice, or another environmental or cultural cause. Cultural and environmental problems include:

Temperature: When it's too warm for cool-season grasses, they often show symptoms of drought. Blades curl, and the lawn becomes yellowish or brown.

Water: If lawns are dry during hot periods, they will go into summer dormancy, turning brown or tan. Dormancy is a healthy reaction to a lack of water. Problems arise when lawns are given just enough water to not go dormant, but not enough water to produce strong roots and shoots. In this state lawns are also susceptible to damage from pests and overuse.

Wear and compaction: Overuse of a lawn can damage grass faster than it can grow. It can also compact soil, pressing air out of the top few inches, causing roots to become shallow and the grass to weaken. At its worst, paths develop where people walk, or the grass under a child's swing becomes bare.

Nutrients: Both over- and underfed lawns are susceptible to problems. Underfed grass grows slowly, has a restricted root system, and is unable to outgrow pest damage. It doesn't have that healthy green sheen and is more often pale green or yellowish. Overfertilized lawns may become succulent and easily damaged.

Mowing: Regularly mowing off more than a third of the leaf blade puts the grass at a great disadvantage. The root system never expands, making it tough for the grass to mine for water and nutrients. The lawn always looks off-color, as it can when using dull mower blades. On uneven ground, mower blades can dig into the dirt.

Light: Most lawn grasses are full-sun plants and do best in bright light. Even shade-tolerant grasses need at least four hours of filtered sunlight a day. Grass that has become so thin that the soil shows through may indicate a lack of light.

Pesticide labels

Pesticides are very effective if used properly but can cause damage when misused. When purchasing a pesticide, look for the pest on the label. If it isn't listed, it is illegal and may be ineffective to use that pesticide for that pest. Also be sure the pesticide is made for your type of grass. Some pesticides for cool-season grasses must not be used on warm-season species. Read and understand the instructions and cautions on the label. Reread the label to refresh your memory every time you apply the pest control.

Using
pest controls

Although diseases, insects, and other inhabitants of the natural world may inflict harm upon a lawn, few of these are devastating. In fact, most pests abandon plants when environmental conditions change. The first step in controlling any lawn pest is to determine exactly what pest you are working with. After identifying the culprit, take steps to control the pest through changes in your cultural or mechanical practices, such as feeding, watering, and mowing. Chemicals should be used as a last result. This pest management philosophy is called integrated pest management, or IPM. It is an environmentally responsible method of controlling pests.

IPM

The heart of IPM is to solve garden problems with methods that are as harmless to the environment as possible but also produce visible improvements.

IPM has been adopted by all agricultural colleges and universities in the United States, and by the extension service—the outreach arm of those colleges. In fact, the philosophy has become so popular that the schools now publish information under the title "IPM" rather than "Pest Control."

The logic of IPM is similar to the logic of medicine. If a doctor discovers you have an elevated cholesterol level during a routine checkup, you will probably be advised to change your diet and start exercising. If that doesn't bring your cholesterol down, drugs might be prescribed. If it

Be smart

Many lawn problems result from poor maintenance or from too much or too little water, fertilizer, shade, or from sweltering heat. Never just automatically spray a pest control on a lawn. If the lawn is suffering from poor care or is weak because its needs aren't being met, a pest control won't help a bit.

Identify the culprit, then if a chemical pest control is called for, read and follow all the directions and cautions on product labels. Using either too much or too little of a product, or applying it at the wrong time, can make problems worse, not to mention waste time and money and harm the environment. Proper maintenance and good nutrition are integral parts of any pest-control program.

worsens and threatens to cause a heart attack, you might have surgery to open your arteries. On the other hand, if the first time you see the doctor is during a heart attack, it is unlikely that diet and exercise will be the cure. You may go straight to surgery.

Similarly IPM tries to solve problems in the least invasive way first. If a problem can be solved by increasing fertilizer frequency, there may be no need to do anything else. But if the problem is serious, or if gentler ways fail, IPM recommends chemical methods.

To control a weed problem like this one, it is important to first consider changing cultural practices or employing mechanical controls before applying an herbicide.

PEST CONTROL METHODS

Insecticides and fungicides are not the only ways to combat insects and diseases. In many cases, they may not even be the best way. Some problems can be solved by changing the environment (such as by thinning a tree to let more light reach the lawn), by changing your cultural practices, by employing mechanical methods, or by using biological agents.

■ *Cultural methods:* Poor or improper lawn care weakens grass and leads to problems. Sometimes, simply changing care tactics—mowing taller, watering correctly, (applying ½ to 1 inch of water twice weekly) or aerating— is all it takes to cure a problem. At other times, however, once the problem has gotten a toehold, improving lawn care isn't enough.

■ *Mechanical methods:* Many problems are solved mechanically, as when weeds are pulled by hand or gophers are trapped with spring traps. Sometimes these are the best ways to solve a problem. In other cases, they might give the appearance of success, but the problem returns quickly, as when you pull a dandelion.

■ *Biological methods:* Biological pest controls involve using agents such as nematodes, bacteria, and other organisms to eliminate and prevent problems. Not many are available for use on lawns. One that is becoming common is endophytes, fungi bred to live within grasses and stop insect pests.

■ *Chemical methods:* Insecticides, fungicides, and herbicides fall in this category. Among them are materials derived from natural substances, such as pyrethrin. A good pest control is one that kills the target pest (insect, disease-causing organism, or weed) without any other effects. Chemical methods should be the last resort when working to control a pest.

Weeds
and control

In lawns, a weed is any plant that disrupts the uniformity of the turf. It could be a readily identifiable broadleaf invader, such as dandelions, or it could be another turfgrass, such as tall fescue in a bluegrass lawn.

Think of weeds as opportunistic raiders that constantly probe your lawn for weaknesses so they can mount an invasion. Weeds that thrive in compacted soil take over where the ground is too compact for good turfgrass growth. Where the lawn doesn't get enough water, drought-resistant weeds move in. Water-loving weeds will invade overwatered and poorly drained lawns. Underfed lawns are open to weeds that thrive in poor soil.

Once weeds have established a stronghold, they invade surrounding territory. By taking more than their share of food and water, they further weaken nearby grass so that they can creep farther.

WEED WEAPONS

■ *Weed seeds:* Seeds are one of the most important weapons in a weed's arsenal. Many weeds—especially annuals—produce copious amounts of seed.

Whenever you disturb soil, you bring new weed seeds to the surface to germinate. That's why it's so important to aerate in the fall and do other soil-disturbing activities when the seed is less likely to germinate.

■ *Runners and spreaders:* Many weeds compete with lawn grasses by spreading from a central point. They do this by growing new plants from their crowns or by sending out runners either above or just below the soil surface. The runners root at intervals and form a new plant.

■ *Underground attack:* Many weeds persist against all efforts to eradicate them because of their underground parts. Dandelions, for example, have a deep, strong taproot dotted with dormant buds. Other weeds, such as nutsedge, pull up easily but leave behind small "nuts" to sprout into new plants.

Grassy weeds subtly disrupt the uniformity of a lawn. They may grow faster than the lawn or have a different color or texture.

■ *Surviving mowing:* To survive in a lawn, the growing points of weedy plants must be lower than the mowing height. Few flower garden weeds move into the lawn because mowing kills them.

■ *Chemical warfare:* Some weeds slow the growth of the lawn around them by emitting toxic chemicals from their roots. This is called allelopathy.

GROUPING WEEDS

Weeds conveniently divide into groups that have traits in common. Weeds in a group can often be controlled with the same methods. Knowing which group a weed falls into helps you select an effective control.

■ *Grassy and broadleaf weeds:* Grassy weeds include grasses such as crabgrass and foxtail, and a couple of relatives of grasses, such as sedges and rushes. Broadleaf weeds are everything else. The sedges are a group of grassy weeds that look like grasses at first glance. You can tell them from grasses by their triangular stems. Sedges generally show up in low, wet areas but may occur almost anywhere lawns grow.

■ *Annual and perennial weeds:* Annual weeds are those that live for up to 12 months, which is not necessarily a calendar year. Perennial weeds live for at least three growing seasons (some gardeners would say they live forever!).

Annual weeds can be further divided into two groups: winter and summer. Summer annual weeds germinate from seed as weather warms in spring and die with the first frost in fall. A few annual weeds die with the first hot weather of summer. These are winter annuals.

Broadleaf weeds include any plant that doesn't look like a grass, such as clover, dandelions, and chickweed.

CONTROL TACTICS

Mowing at a high setting helps to control annual weeds. Another tactic is to prevent seed germination. Because annual seeds have a short life, keeping them from germinating stops the weeds dead.

There are two ways to prevent germination. The first is to not let seeds form in the first place. Whenever a weed produces seed, you will do battle again the following year. But if you kill annual weeds before seed is set, you won't.

The second method is to use preemergence herbicides. These are compounds that kill germinating seedlings already in the soil but don't harm growing plants.

Perennial weeds can be more difficult to control than annual weeds. Most perennials don't make as many seeds each year as annuals do, but keeping their seeds from germinating isn't enough to kill them. Some perennials (and some annuals too) grow roots and start new plants wherever their stems touch the ground. This creeping habit can cause them to form large mats that crowd out lawn grasses. Perennial grassy weeds are the most difficult to control. Any control method you use on them will also affect the lawn because they are so similar to lawn grasses.

Controlling
weeds

Several approaches are possible in controlling weeds. Using an herbicide is only one of them. Often, a good weed-control plan requires two or three methods.

CULTURAL CONTROLS

With cultural control you use management practices such as irrigation, fertilization, and mowing to strengthen the lawn grasses and create conditions that discourage the growth of weeds.

The best weed control is a well-fed, thick, healthy turf. Properly managed grass out-competes most weeds. The instructions for management practices given in earlier chapters tell you what conditions favor the lawn grasses. The more you can create the conditions they prefer, the stronger and thicker the grass will be and the fewer weeds the lawn will have. In addition to mowing, fertilizing, and irrigating, you can also employ these cultural controls.

■ *Mechanical control:* Pulling or digging out weeds works well with some weeds, especially if there are only a few. Consider this method for annual weeds and perennial weeds that don't resprout from underground parts— taproots, rhizomes, bulbs, and the like. Hand-pulling can control seedlings, even species that have persistent underground parts, if those parts haven't had time to form yet. For mechanical controls to be successful, frequent careful inspections are necessary, at least at the time the weed seeds are sprouting, and you must pull every weed that starts.

Selecting herbicides

Herbicides generally work for a class of weeds, with most weeds in the class controlled by the same group of herbicides.

■ **Annual grasses:** Control annual grasses with preemergence herbicides applied to the soil before the weed germinates. Timing is critical with these herbicides—they are not effective once the seed has germinated and formed a root. These herbicides are effective for a limited time: from a few weeks to three to four months, depending on the herbicide, soil type, and weather conditions.

■ **Perennial grasses:** Perennial grasses are the most difficult weeds to control. Once they're established, it's generally necessary to use nonselective herbicides, which also kill the lawn, to control them. Spot treat individual patches of these weeds. Glyphosate (Roundup®) is the herbicide most widely used to control perennial grasses.

■ **Broadleaf weeds:** Both perennial and annual broadleaf weeds can be controlled by selective postemergence broadleaf herbicides.

■ *Biological control:* Research is being conducted on using naturally occurring, living biological organisms that kill certain weeds without damaging the grass. This approach is not yet ready for the market but shows promise. The biggest limitation is the selectivity with which these organisms kill plants. Finding organisms that kill a wide variety of weeds without killing the grass will be difficult. Keep an eye open for this developing control.

HERBICIDES

The most commonly used method for weed control—because it's so effective—is chemical. Chemicals that kill plants are called herbicides. Two basic types of herbicides exist, each with its own action and method of use.

■ *Postemergence herbicides:* These kill existing weeds. They fall into four categories:

Contact herbicides: Horticultural oil and herbicidal soaps are examples. These herbicides kill all plant tissue they come in contact with. These materials give quick results, with the plant wilting in just a few hours and appearing dead by the next day. Unfortunately, only tissue that is actually contacted dies, which means that the weed can resprout from the roots and other underground parts.

Systemic herbicides: *Systemic* refers to the fact that the herbicide moves throughout the plant's system before killing the plant, so the whole plant, including underground parts, dies.

Selective herbicides: Selective herbicides take advantage of differences in the biological workings among plant groups to kill some and not others. The most common selective herbicides used in lawns—the ones contained in weed-and-feed fertilizers—kill broadleaf weeds but not grasses.

Nonselective herbicides: These herbicides kill everything they are sprayed on—lawn grasses as well as weeds. Apply them carefully. They are generally used against perennial grassy weeds, which cannot be killed with selective herbicides.

Nonselective herbicides are sold as ready-to-use sprays and in containers that shoot jets of foam that can be aimed accurately and mark which weeds you've already sprayed. These herbicides are also available in concentrated form. Glyphosate (Roundup®) is the most popular herbicide in this group.

■ *Preemergence herbicides:* This type of herbicide kills seeds as they germinate but has no effect on growing plants. It is called *preemergence* because it kills weeds before they emerge from the ground. (All others are postemergence.)

Preemergence herbicides are effective against annual weeds. It's possible to control annual weeds with preemergence herbicides alone. You may also see some reduction in the number of perennial weeds.

Weed profiles

ANNUAL BLUEGRASS

Cool-season winter annual; some strains are perennial. Seed germinates from late summer to late fall and grows rapidly in spring, especially if lawn is fertilized then. Most serious in cool, wet climates where lawns are mowed closely and in poorly drained, overwatered, and compacted soils. It usually dies in early summer when temperatures rise.

■ *Immediate control:* Preemergence herbicides control only annual strains.

■ *Prevention:* Best control is to mow at a height of 2½ inches or taller. Aerate compacted areas. Time irrigations far enough apart that the surface of the ground dries. If you use a preemergence herbicide, it should be applied in late summer or early fall, about the time the nights turn cool; avoid using if you plan to reseed the lawn in fall.

BARNYARD GRASS

Summer annual with shallow root system. Reproduces by seed. The natural growth habit is upright, but when mowed it forms ground-hugging mats. Usually found in poorly managed lawns of low fertility. Often found in sandy soil.

■ *Immediate control:* Kill mats by spot treating with a nonselective herbicide. Repeat the treatment two more times at intervals of 7 to 10 days, until plants die.

■ *Prevention:* Apply a preemergence herbicide in early spring, two weeks before the last expected frost. Improve soil fertility and maintain a dense, healthy lawn; this weed is not very competitive in well-maintained lawns.

ANNUAL BLUEGRASS
(Poa annua)
■ Pale green, lighter in color than Kentucky bluegrass
■ Turns yellow and dies with onset of hot weather
■ Abundant seed heads, which are at same height as the grass; give whitish cast to the lawn
■ North America, especially cool, wet regions, Hawaii

BARNYARD GRASS
(Echinochloa crusgalli)
■ Distinctive seed head, with seeds on six to eight segments
■ 1- to 3-foot-long reddish purple stems
■ Smooth leaves, prominent midrib
■ North America

BROADLEAF PLANTAIN

Broadleaf perennial. Forms a rosette, with rounded leaves lying along the surface of the ground. A slender seed stalk stands tall above the lawn in midsummer. There are many local names for broadleaf plantain, among them black seed and Rugel's plantain.

■ *Immediate control:*
Broadleaf plantain is easily controlled by standard selective postemergence broadleaf herbicides.

■ *Prevention:* Treating it in fall usually prevents it from returning the following year.

BROADLEAF PLANTAIN *(Plantago rugelii)*
■ Central rosette of 2- to 10-inch-long, egg-shaped leaves
■ Small flower heads held high above the lawn
■ North America, east of the Rockies

BUCKHORN PLANTAIN

Broadleaf perennial. Buckhorn plantain is closely related to broadleaf plantain. It differs by having narrow, pointed leaves and seeds that develop just at the tip of the seed stalk rather than extending 2 inches or more down the stalk. Buckhorn plantain takes a long time to become established and is usually associated with older turf areas, like cemeteries or older park areas.

■ *Immediate control:* Treat the whole lawn or spot treat it with selective postemergence broadleaf herbicide. Don't mow for five days before treatment or two days afterward. Late fall is the best time to control buckhorn plantain; spring is second best.

■ *Prevention:* Even the best herbicides and combination of herbicides may fail to kill buckhorn plantain. Persistence is the best approach.

BUCKHORN PLANTAIN *(Plantago lanceolata)*
■ Central rosette of narrow, lance-shaped leaves
■ Flowers held a foot above the rosette of leaves at the tip of the flower stalk
■ North America and Hawaii

Weed profiles
continued

CANADA THISTLE

Broadleaf perennial. Spreads by rhizomes and seed. Large, spiny leaves. Several thistles occur in lawns, but Canada thistle is the most common through all of the United States and Canada. When mowed, it takes on a rosette growth pattern like that of a dandelion, with its deeply lobed leaves growing along the ground's surface.

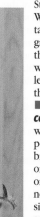

■ *Immediate control:* Spot treat with a selective postemergence broadleaf herbicide or paint glyphosate on the leaves. If necessary, repeat after six weeks. Treatments are most effective in early spring or late summer.

**CANADA THISTLE
(Cirsium arvense)**
■ Forms close-cropped rosettes in mowed lawns
■ Deeply lobed leaves with spines on edges
■ Dies back to the ground with the first frost
■ North America, primarily the North

■ *Prevention:* Spot treat seedlings with glyphosate.

CRABGRASS

Summer annual. Plants spread rapidly, by seed in spring and by rooting stems all summer. Seed lies dormant over winter and sprouts in spring. Crabgrass out-competes cool-season lawns during hot weather. When a lawn thins out from insects, disease, low fertility, drought, low mowing, or poor drainage, crabgrass is one of the first weeds to invade.

■ *Immediate control:* Although preventive measures are best, you can kill crabgrass with a postemergence weed killer labeled for it. Older plants are harder to kill; repeat the treatment twice at four- to seven-day intervals.

■ *Prevention:* Apply preemergence controls in late winter or early spring, about the time that forsythia blossoms drop. Follow good cultural practices; crabgrass is less of a problem in thick, healthy lawns.

DANDELION

Broadleaf perennial. Reproduces by seed. One of the most universally recognized lawn weeds, with yellow flowers in spring, followed by the fluffy white seed heads that are a favorite of children. Its deeply lobed leaves radiate from a central growing point to form a rosette. This is a highly variable plant; it is common to find dandelions having rounded leaves with a few pointed extensions at their base that point back into the center of the rosette. Dandelions are highly competitive with lawns, and even the best-managed lawn may have some. The deep taproot makes dandelions difficult to control by pulling or cutting; the weed generally comes back quickly if even a small piece of the root remains in the soil.

■ *Immediate control:* Easy to control by treating the lawn or spot treating with a selective postemergence broadleaf herbicide. Lawns are easily kept dandelion free with a single, well-timed application. The best time to treat for dandelions and other perennial broadleaf weeds is in the fall, when they are storing carbohydrates (or food) in their roots for next spring's growth. In fall, the plants readily translocate the herbicide to underground plant parts. The second best time to treat for dandelions is in late spring.

■ *Prevention:* Be vigilant; spray dandelions with a selective postemergence broadleaf herbicide as they appear. Treat in fall to prevent a spring crop.

CRABGRASS *(Digitaria* spp.)
■ Thick, heavy stems
■ Seed head like a crow's foot or fingers, thus the name *Digitaria*
■ Light green leaves
■ Stems may root at joints
■ Rolled vernation
■ North America, except Northwest

SMOOTH CRABGRASS
(Digitaria ischaemum)
■ Smooth leaves without hairs
■ Often found in lawns with large hairy crabgrass
■ Seed heads that branch from multiple locations on leafstalk

LARGE HAIRY CRABGRASS
(Digitaria sanguinalis)
■ Leaves covered with fine hairs
■ Seed heads that branch from multiple locations on leafstalk

TROPICAL CRABGRASS
(Digitaria bicornis)
■ Similar to large hairy crabgrass, but with seed heads that branch from a single central point
■ Gulf Coast and Florida

SOUTHERN CRABGRASS
(Digitaria ciliaris)
■ Similar to large hairy crabgrass but occurs in warmer regions
■ Warm regions, from the Midwest to Mexico

DANDELION
(Taraxacum officinale)
■ Bright yellow flowers
■ Rosette of jagged leaves
■ White puffball seed heads
■ North America and Hawaii

Weed profiles

continued

GOOSEGRASS

Summer annual. Reproduces by seed that begins germinating in spring, two to three weeks later than crabgrass, and continues germinating into midsummer. It is frequently mistaken for crabgrass and is sometimes called silver crabgrass. Grows extensive root system that is difficult to pull. Most often invades thin areas of the lawn where soil is compacted and infertile.

■ *Immediate control:* Kill clumps by spot treating with a nonselective herbicide. After seven days, remove the weed. It will still be green, but the roots will have been killed and will not resprout. Reduce soil compaction, then reseed or resod.

■ *Prevention:* Apply a preemergence herbicide in late spring or early summer. Maintain a healthy, dense lawn.

GOOSEGRASS (Eleusine indica)
■ Forms rosettes resembling spikes of a wheel
■ Smooth, flat-stemmed, dark green leaves 2 to 10 inches long, silvery and hairy at the base
■ Stems do not root at the stem joints
■ Vernation: folded
■ North America (except Northwest), Hawaii

Crabgrass vs. goosegrass

■ New leaves of crabgrass emerge rolled, whereas new goosegrass leaves emerge folded.
■ Goosegrass stems do not root at the stem joints; those of crabgrass may.
■ Leaves of goosegrass are usually darker green than those of crabgrass.
■ Goosegrass seed heads are thicker.

GROUND IVY

Persistent broadleaf perennial. Also called creeping Charlie, ground ivy has rounded leaves and extensive runners that can out-compete most lawn grasses. It is well adapted to shade and, in fact, was once recommended as a shade garden plant, from where it moved into the lawn. Ground ivy will spread rapidly into full sun, however, and readily becomes a serious weed problem.

■ *Immediate control:* Treat with a selective herbicide labeled for ground ivy. The best time to apply it is fall.

■ *Prevention:* If ground ivy grows in the neighbors' lawns, it will probably take regular treatments to keep it out of yours. Its aggressive, spreading runners quickly reinfest the lawn, and the problem usually returns within a year of treatment. The best approach is persistence, and convincing your neighbors to do the same.

NIMBLEWILL

Warm-season perennial with shallow roots. Reproduces readily by seed and by stems that root at the lower nodes. Seeds are produced August to October and lie dormant over winter to sprout in late spring. Plant tops become dormant in fall and begin growth again the following spring. Invades moist lawns, gardens, and unplanted areas with rich, gravelly soil.

■ *Immediate control:* No selective herbicide. Kill with a single application of glyphosate (Roundup®). Nimblewill is easiest to kill as a seedling, from late spring to early summer. To eradicate it completely where it has invaded a lawn, the entire area must be killed with a nonselective herbicide followed by reestablishment of the lawn with sod. Nimblewill readily comes back from seed before a new lawn can become established by seed. Sod keeps the seeds from sprouting.

■ *Prevention:* Before it has had a chance to produce seeds, hand pull from garden beds and other areas of open soil near the lawn.

GROUND IVY (Glechoma hederacea)
■ Nickel to quarter size, scalloped round leaves
■ Leaves paired opposite each other along square stem
■ Purplish blue flowers in spring and early summer
■ Distinct odor
■ North America, except Southwest

NIMBLEWILL (Muhlenbergia schreberi)
■ Spreading habit, wiry appearance
■ Wiry stems grow out and then up (to 10 inches tall).
■ Bluish green leaves that turn whitish tan with fall frost
■ Each seed has a small hair (an awn) at its tip.
■ Found throughout North America east of the Rocky Mountains

Weed profiles
continued

ORCHARDGRASS
(Dactylis glomerata)
- Wide, smooth leaves
- Grows faster than the lawn
- North America and Hawaii

ORCHARDGRASS

Cool-season perennial. It often shows up in tall fescue or Kentucky bluegrass lawns grown from bargain seed. It is a bluish green, coarse-textured bunchgrass common in the cooler parts of the Midwest and Northeast. Orchardgrass grows quickly, rising an inch or more above the lawn within a few days of mowing.

■ *Immediate control:* There is no selective chemical control. Small patches can be removed by digging out and replacing the soil. Or spot treat with glyphosate. If the infestation is extensive, kill the entire lawn, then reestablish it.

■ *Prevention:* Dense, healthy turf is the best guard against orchardgrass becoming established. Avoid introducing it in sod, the root ball of new trees and shrubs, and inexpensive seed mixes.

PROSTRATE KNOTWEED

Summer annual. Reproduces from numerous seeds, which germinate as soon as the soil warms in early spring. Sometimes mistaken for young crabgrass when it germinates; it emerges six to eight weeks before crabgrass. This weed cannot find a toehold in a vigorous, dense turf, but it can be a problem in lawns of low fertility and compacted soil, especially along driveways and in paths cut through lawns. It sometimes is found in newly established lawns.

■ *Immediate control:* Treat the lawn with a selective broadleaf herbicide in early spring when the seedlings are still young. Repeated treatments may be necessary.

■ *Prevention:* Relieve soil compaction by aerating, diverting traffic from the grass, or placing stepping-stones or paths where people walk. Follow a regular fertilization program and sound maintenance practices to maintain a healthy and vigorous lawn.

PROSTRATE KNOTWEED
(Polygonum aviculare)
- Low mats, up to 2 feet wide
- Tiny, greenish-white flowers, June to November
- Smooth, 1-inch, oval leaves
- Leaves alternate along wiry stems
- No milky sap at end of cut stem
- From southern Canada south

PURSLANE

Summer annual. Reproduces by seed that may remain viable in the soil for many years and sprout in warm weather when brought to the surface by aerating. Forms thick mats; stems root wherever they touch soil. Thrives in hot, dry weather and is seldom found in spring. Plants die with the first frost. Purslane has difficulty becoming established in healthy, vigorous lawns. Stems and leaves store water, enabling the plant to survive drought and to grow in cracks in sidewalks and driveways. Plants pulled and allowed to lie on the soil will reroot.

■ *Immediate control:* Kill with selective postemergence broadleaf herbicides. If the infestation is small, hand pull plants. Dispose of pulled plants to prevent rerooting. Wait three to four weeks before seeding bare areas after application.

■ *Prevention:* Follow good lawn-management practices to maintain a healthy, vigorous lawn. A regular fertilization schedule combined with adequate watering will keep purslane at bay.

PURSLANE *(Portulaca oleracea)*
■ Low-growing mats
■ Thick, succulent, reddish-brown stems
■ Thick, fleshy, wedge-shaped leaves
■ Occasionally blooms with small, yellow flowers
■ Found throughout North America but most prevalent east of the Rocky Mountains

QUACKGRASS

Cool-season perennial spreading by rhizomes. It spreads by seed and rhizomes. Small parts of a rhizome left in the soil when the weed is pulled will quickly grow into new plants. Tolerates nearly all types of soil; competitive with all plants. It can quickly take over newly planted lawns.

■ *Immediate control:* Quackgrass is difficult to kill. All parts of the rhizome must be killed or it will quickly reinfest the lawn.

If the entire lawn is infested, the lawn will need to be killed and another reestablished.

If only isolated areas are infested, kill them and patch those spots with sod. Let the quackgrass grow 4 to 6 inches tall, then spray it with a nonselective systemic herbicide. Regrowth is likely; if it occurs, repeat the treatment. Reestablish the lawn with sod rather than seed, because quackgrass rhizomes have difficulty surfacing through dense, newly laid sod.

■ *Prevention:* Dense, healthy grass discourages quackgrass. Check sod and the root ball of new trees to avoid introducing quackgrass in your yard. When seeding new lawns, purchase high-quality seed.

QUACKGRASS *(Elymus repens)*
■ Hollow stems with wheatlike spikes at tips
■ Narrow bluish green blades, rough on upper surface
■ Pair of long, clawlike, clasping auricles
■ North America, except South; most prevalent in cool climates and along West Coast

Weed profiles
continued

SMOOTH BROME

Cool-season perennial with shallow, fibrous roots and short rhizomes. Produces many seeds, which are spread to lawns by birds or wind. Seed germinates in fall or early spring. Most troublesome in areas with dry, sandy, or gravelly soil.

■ *Immediate control:* Individual plants may be pulled by hand. No selective chemical control; the entire lawn must be killed to eliminate it. Use a single application of glyphosate prior to reestablishing the lawn.

■ *Prevention:* Weed early in the season and frequently to prevent smooth brome from becoming established in the lawn.

SMOOTH BROME *(Bromus inermis)*
■ Smooth stems, 6 to 24 inches tall
■ 2- to 6-inch-long, light green leaves
■ Sheath like a V-neck sweater
■ Drooping purple seed heads, spring
■ Plants purplish tan at maturity
■ Most noticeable in spring and fall
■ North America, except Southeast

SMUTGRASS

Perennial. A tufted bunchgrass that forms deep-rooted clumps in lawns. The blades are less than ½ inch wide and taper to a point. This weed is common in the Southeast and is particularly a problem in bahiagrass lawns.

■ *Immediate control:* Use a postemergence herbicide on warm-season lawns.

■ *Long-term prevention:* Use a preemergence herbicide labeled for smutgrass. Dense, healthy turf discourages establishment of this weed. Ensure that new sod or the root ball of new trees and shrubs don't harbor smutgrass. Use only high-quality seed.

SMUTGRASS
(*Sporobulus indicus*)
■ Coarse-textured clumps
■ Black fungus on ripening seeds
■ Leaf blades are flat at the base and rounded toward the tip
■ Common in the southeastern United States and the tropics

TALL FESCUE

Warm-season clumping perennial. Very coarse blades originate from a central point. Although some types of tall fescue have short rhizomes, most are bunchgrasses that form clumps in the lawn.

■ *Immediate control:* Spot treat with glyphosate or have a professional treat your lawn with a restricted herbicide, not available to homeowners to selectively kill tall fescue (in Kentucky bluegrass lawns only).

■ *Prevention:* Spot treat with glyphosate (Roundup®) whenever a clump appears. New clumps don't resprout after pulling.

TALL FESCUE
(Festuca arundinacea)
■ Coarse blades to ½ inch wide, ribbed on top and smooth on bottom
■ North America and Hawaii

TIMOTHY

Cool-season, deep-rooted perennial. Forms distinct clumps that do not spread. A turf-type timothy is used as a lawn in Europe but not in North America.

■ *Immediate control:* No selective herbicide. Kill with a single application of glyphosate (Roundup®), followed by seeding to reestablish the lawn.

■ *Prevention:* Dense, healthy turf will discourage timothy from becoming established. Avoid introducing it in new sod or the root ball of new trees and shrubs. Use only high-quality seed mixes.

TIMOTHY
(Phleum pratense)
■ Coarse texture that stands out
■ Broad, bulbous structure at the base of plants
■ Distinctive seed head, similar to foxtail but tighter, more compact
■ North America and Hawaii

Weed profiles

continued

WHITE CLOVER

Broadleaf perennial. Has white flowers from spring to fall. In the 1940s and 1950s, white clover was often added to Kentucky bluegrass seed mixes. This has resulted in it being one of the most widely distributed weeds in cool-season lawns in the United States. It attracts bees, posing a hazard to barefooted people. It is most prolific in wet soil.

■ *Immediate control:* Treat the lawn with a postemergence broadleaf herbicide or weed-and-feed labeled for clover. Fall is the best time.

■ *Prevention:* Once cleaned out of a lawn, it is not likely to return. Spot treat any plants that do appear.

WHITE CLOVER (Trifolium repens)
■ Shamrock-shaped leaves with three round leaflets at the top of 2- to 4-inch-long stalks that sprout directly from the base of the plant
■ ½-inch clusters of white or pinkish flowers from June to September
■ Attracts many bees
■ North America and Hawaii

WILD ONION AND WILD GARLIC

Wild onion and wild garlic reproduce mostly by bulbs and bulblets. Both soft and hard bulblets are formed underground. The soft bulblets germinate in autumn; the hard bulblets remain dormant over winter and germinate the following spring or in summer. Both species also reproduce by seed and by bulblets produced at the tips

Is it wild onion or wild garlic?

■ Wild garlic leaf is hollow and round in cross section. It has a strong garlic odor. Bulb has a membranous coat.
■ Wild onion leaf is not hollow and is more flat in cross section. It has a strong onion odor when crushed. Bulb has a fibrous coat.

of some of their leaves. Wild garlic and wild onion spread rapidly through lawns, especially in thin, open turf that is not well-maintained.

■ *Immediate control:* Wild garlic and wild onion are difficult to control. Hand digging is impractical because any bulbs left behind sprout into new plants and quickly multiply. Apply a selective broadleaf herbicide as the leaves emerge in spring or anytime the plants are actively growing. Repeat the application in two weeks. Because plants can regrow from the bulbs and the bulbs sprout at different times of year, repeat the treatments annually for the next two or three years.

■ *Prevention:* Frequent mowing in spring helps reduce the vigor and spread of these weeds.

WILD VIOLET

Broadleaf perennial. Violets have an attractive purple flower and are not always objectionable in a lawn. The plants have shiny leaves with a waxy coating that makes penetration by herbicides difficult. They often survive when all other weeds in the lawn have been controlled. Violets are usually associated with shaded areas where the turf is thin from lack of light, but they will also grow in full sun in a well-watered lawn.

■ *Immediate control:* Apply postemergence broadleaf herbicides labeled for wild violet.

■ *Prevention:* Hand pull or spot treat seedlings with glyphosate. Spread a preemergence herbicide in early spring. In mild-winter areas with severe infestations, repeat the treatment in late fall.

WILD ONION (Allium canadense) AND WILD GARLIC (Allium vineale)

■ Pungent odor to crushed leaves

■ Leaves joined at the lower half of the main stem just above where it emerges from an underground bulb

■ Greenish-purple or white flowers; the same height as the leaves

■ Common in Canada and much of the U.S., especially the East Coast and the Southeast

WILD VIOLETS (Viola spp.)

■ Grows from a central point to form broad, low rosettes

■ Rounded, heart-shaped leaves to 2 inches long

■ Violet, sometimes yellow or white, flowers in spring

■ North America and Hawaii

Insect pests and controls

A healthy lawn is a good defense against insect pests. To a certain extent, it protects itself against insect damage, although it doesn't do as good a job against insects as it does against weeds and diseases. However, a healthy lawn can endure a lot of insect feeding without showing it. And once the insects are gone, a healthy lawn makes a quicker recovery from the damage than a lawn that isn't healthy.

Insecticides are the most effective control of insect pests in lawns. Certain bacteria and nematodes are parasites or predators of insects, and research has demonstrated their effectiveness. However, they have not proven practical to use as pest controls in lawns.

Whichever material or control method you use, the most important aspect of achieving success is to apply it when the insect is most vulnerable. For example, as insects grow larger, thicker exoskeletons, they are better able to tolerate pesticides (it takes more pesticide or stronger pesticides to kill them) and become more difficult to control.

Other insects may spend portions of their lives in protected locations within the plant or the soil. Insects feeding on grass blades are relatively easy to control. Getting a pest that burrows into the soil involves understanding exactly where the pest resides, when it will be in a spot that is easy to reach, and when it is most vulnerable to insecticides.

Chinch bugs ($\frac{1}{8}$-inch-long) suck juices from grass plants. They are easy to control if diagnosed early.

Identifying insect damage

Insects usually damage lawns by their feeding. Grubs eat roots, billbugs eat the crown of a grass plant, and sod webworms eat the grass blades. It is important to properly diagnose damage to effectively control the insects. When you suspect insect damage, follow these steps for diagnosis.

■ **Look for insects:** Get down on your hands and knees and look for insects on the grass plants. A hand lens is often helpful to see the tiny insects. The insect profiles, beginning on page 64, explain what to look for and where to look.

■ **Examine turf damage:** Insects often do their damage and leave. Signs of their feeding may be the only way to identify the culprit. For example, grubs sever the root system so that the grass easily breaks away below the crown, where the roots have been cut.

■ **Keep track of damage:** In sunny areas, insect damage tends to recur at about the same time each year. If you have problems with an insect one year, mark your calendar and look for it at the same time the next year.

INSECT DAMAGE

Insects usually damage lawns by their feeding. Grubs eat roots, billbugs the crown, and sod webworms the grass blades. This type of damage is called direct damage.

Indirect damage occurs when animals such as skunks, raccoons, and armadillos dig up areas looking for insects to feed on. Indirect damage can be worse than direct damage and can occur even when insect populations are such that you are unaware of the insects' presence.

Insect damage may look the same as damage caused by drought, disease, or other harmful conditions. The surest way of diagnosing the problem when you suspect insect damage is to look for the insects themselves. Examine the turf; turn up a patch of grass and examine the soil to find the culprit. Insects often do their damage, then leave. Signs of their feeding may be the only way to identify the pest. Examine the quality of the turf.

Skunks, raccoons, and other animals destroy lawns while digging for soil-dwelling insects. The indirect damage may be worse than that of the insect.

MONITOR INSECTS

Insect damage tends to recur at about the same time each year. If you have problems with an insect one year, mark your calendar to start looking for it at the same time the following year. This will help especially for insects that are hard to spot before they cause damage. Then you can treat for them before any significant damage is done, when the insect is young and easier to control.

One way to monitor lawn insects is with a flush test, which uses soap to drive insects to the surface, where you can see them. This test helps detect cutworms, mole crickets, army worms, sod webworms, chinch bugs, and billbug adults.

Mix 2 tablespoons of dish detergent (lemon-scented works best) in 2 gallons of water in a watering can. Sprinkle the mixture on a square-yard section of lawn where you suspect the insects. If present, they'll come to the surface within five to 10 minutes, irritated by the soap.

CHOOSE AN INSECTICIDE

If insect populations progress to an intolerable point— the pests are causing excessive damage—it's time to call on insecticides. Choose an insecticide that is specifically labeled for the pest you are trying to control and apply the product as directed on the package.

Insect profiles

WHITE GRUBS

White grubs are the larvae of several species of beetles. The adults do not feed on grass but may damage ornamental plants.

Extensive damage occurs when grubs feed on grass roots in the top layer of soil, 1 to 3 inches below the crown. The grass wilts and dies from lack of water. Birds and other animals may further damage the lawn as they search for grubs to eat.

If you suspect grubs, grasp the grass and lift. It will break away at the roots. It almost rolls up like a rug. If damage is recent, you may see grubs on the soil surface. More likely, they have burrowed deep into the soil where they are out of sight.

The species of white grubs that attack turf vary by region. June beetles (also called June bugs or May beetles) are common throughout the United States; masked chafers are prevalent in the Midwest; Japanese beetles predominate in the East and the Midwest.

Other species, including European chafer, Asiatic beetle, and green June beetle, are less common but do significant damage where they are found.

■ *Control:* White grub control can be difficult. Once you see damage, it's often too late to control the current population, but you can prevent future damage.

Newer grub controls have a season-long residual effect, so that one application takes care of all grubs, no matter when they feed. Apply the control in May, June, or July. It does not affect the adults but ensures you have a layer of protection in place before the eggs hatch and the grubs start to feed in late summer.

Grub tip

Grub feeding does not directly kill the lawn. Drought stress brought on by their feeding kills it. Grub damage is most apparent during dry periods after the grubs have done their damage.

June beetle

Japanese beetle

European chafer

Asiatic beetle

WHITE GRUB SYMPTOMS
■ Irregular patches of wilted brown grass
■ Damaged areas can be rolled up like a carpet, exposing fat, 1/4- to 1-inch-long white grubs with six legs; if you don't see them, sift through the top 2 inches of soil, for they may have burrowed deeper.
■ The first sign of grubs may be holes in the lawn from birds, skunks, or raccoons digging; all make triangular holes with sod pulled aside.
■ All of North America, several species

SOD WEBWORMS

Sod webworms chew on grass blades just above the crown—in effect, scalping the lawn. They get their name from web-lined tunnels, where the larvae (worms) retreat during the day.

The worms are smooth, green or light brown caterpillars about an inch long with rows of spots on their bodies. Birds eat them, and flocks are sometimes seen on infested lawns. The adult webworms, also called lawn moths, fly up from the lawn as you mow.

The adults fly over lawns in a zigzag pattern, dropping their eggs in flight. There are two egg-laying peaks—one in June and one in August.

■ *Control:* Watch for flights of moths in June and August. Treat two weeks after their flight peaks—their numbers will dwindle, with fewer moths observed one evening than the previous. This is when the larvae are just becoming active.

Webworms are surface feeders and are easy to kill with insecticides if the problem is diagnosed early enough. However, they often go unrecognized until considerable damage has been done. Apply granular insect controls, that provide control for up to six weeks, or spray with a contact insecticide labeled for sod webworms as soon as you see damage. Mow and water the lawn the day before treating. Treat in the evening, as the larvae become active. Don't water for a couple of days after spraying.

SOD WEBWORM ADULTS
- Night-flying
- White to tan or brown
- Snoutlike projection from the head
- When the moths are at rest, their wings wrap around the body to form a tube.

SOD WEBWORM LARVAE
- ¼- to ¾-inch-long, light brown, green, or gray worms with black spots
- Found in silky white tubes nestled in the soil during the day

Observation pays off

Watch for signs of damage to your lawn or—even better—the egg-laying adults themselves. With insects, as with other things that damage a lawn, solving the problem early is not only easier, it ensures less damage is done. Look for moths flying from your lawn as you mow. Watch for billbugs crossing a sidewalk or driveway in the evening. Keep an eye out for other pests. If you can kill the adults before they lay eggs, the lawn may never suffer damage.

Insect profiles

continued

CUTWORM SYMPTOMS

- Grass blades are chewed unevenly along the edges in early or late summer.
- Seedling may be chewed off near the ground.
- When a section of turf is peeled back, larvae may be found in the thatch.
- Bird damage may be evident where birds scratch to feed on the larvae.
- Found in all of North America

CUTWORM LARVAE

- Larvae are 1½- to 2-inch-long, thick-bodied gray, brown, or black worms.
- Larvae curl up and lie still when disturbed.

BLACK CUTWORM adults are dark moths, which you often see fluttering around lights in summer. They have bands or stripes on their forewings.

CUTWORMS

Like sod webworms, cutworms are moth larvae. They hide in thatch during the day and emerge at night to feed, chewing off grass blades close to the ground. Severe damage on mature lawns is rare, but cutworms may riddle a newly seeded lawn with damage.

Cutworms are primarily a problem in early and late summer but can damage lawns throughout the growing season. Once established in spring, several generations can hatch and damage lawns before they die out in the fall.

■ *Control:* Because cutworms are surface feeders, insecticides easily control them. Use a granular product or spray liquid materials in the evening when cutworms are most active. Repeat if damage continues.

BILLBUGS

Adult billbugs are about ½-inch-long weevils. A type of beetle, weevils have a long, curved snout that digs into plant tissue and eats holes in it.

Female billbugs burrow into sheath tissue just above the grass crown to lay eggs. The hollow sheaths protect the eggs until they hatch. Billbug larvae, which look like tiny white grubs, feed in the crown for a while, then move into the soil, where they feed on roots. Billbugs damage lawns in midsummer when the grass is under stress from heat and drought.

Use the "tug test" to identify billbugs. If they are the cause of the damage, the dead grass will break away at the crown as you pull on it. The severed ends of the stems have a sandy material (called frass). Digging near the damage may reveal billbug larvae or pupae, although damage lasts long after the insects are gone. Older larvae are sometimes found with white grubs.

■ *Control:* The key to controlling billbugs is to kill the adults before they can lay eggs. A single insecticide application at the right time usually gives good protection. However, seeing the adults and deciding when to treat can be difficult, even for experts. Begin monitoring for adults in late April to mid-May. The slow-moving adult weevils may be seen crossing driveways after dark. Your local extension service can also tell you if the adults are active.

Apply a grub control that is also labeled for billbugs. Mow the lawn before treating, then irrigate with ½ inch of water to wash the insecticide down to the root level.

Billbug symptoms

- Grass turns brown and dies in expanding, often circular patches.
- Damage may not become apparent until nearby lawns recover from summer stress.
- Dead grass breaks away at the crown when grasped and pulled.
- The hollowed-out stems have a sawdust-like material at the severed ends.
- Digging near damaged crowns may reveal billbug larvae or pupae; damage remains long after the insects are gone.
- In May and October, $\frac{1}{8}$- to $\frac{1}{4}$-inch-long, slow-moving black weevils may be seen crossing sidewalks and driveways.
- All of North America, several species

BLUEGRASS BILLBUG is a pest of cool-season grasses, especially Kentucky bluegrass. Adults overwinter in brush piles and window wells.

HUNTING BILLBUG is a pest of warm-season grasses.

BILLBUG LARVAE
- White, fat, and humpbacked
- $\frac{1}{8}$ to $\frac{1}{4}$ inch long
- Brown heads, no legs

MOLE CRICKETS

Mole crickets feed on grass roots, but their major damage comes from their movements through the soil. They tunnel near the soil surface with strong forelegs, loosening the soil and uprooting plants, which dry out.

They are most prevalent in the Southeast, from North Carolina to east Texas. Bahiagrass and bermudagrass are the preferred grasses, but the insects also feed on St. Augustinegrass, zoysiagrass, and centipedegrass.

Adults migrate to new burrows twice a year, from March to July and again in November and December. They lay eggs from April to midsummer; eggs hatch in June or July. Nymphs feed from midsummer into October or through the winter in some regions.

Control: Chemical control of mole crickets is difficult because they tunnel deeply into the soil where insecticides cannot reach them. Several insecticides are labeled for these insects. The key is to water in the insecticide thoroughly.

Treat the lawn in June or July, after the eggs hatch and before the young nymphs cause much damage. Water the lawn well if it isn't already wet. Treat late in the day, then follow label directions as to how much water to use to wash the insecticide into the soil. Do not water again for 36 hours. Treatments are effective for a couple of weeks, killing new nymphs that hatch during that time. If damage continues, treat again in late summer to early fall.

MOLE CRICKET SYMPTOMS
- Small mounds of soil are scattered on the soil surface.
- Lawn feels spongy underfoot.
- Large areas of the grass turn brown and die.
- North Carolina, through Florida, to the Texas Gulf Coast

Insect profiles

continued

CHINCH BUGS

Chinch bugs suck juices from grass plants. As they feed, they inject toxins into the plant. It takes many chinch bugs to damage a lawn, but they have an incredibly high reproductive rate. Populations can grow to hundreds—even as many as 1,000—per square foot.

They prefer to feed on grass growing in full sun; they avoid shady spots. Often their damage outlines the shade patterns of trees in the lawn.

Eggs hatch into tiny reddish nymphs with cream-colored bands around their midsection. The nymphs go through a number of instars before becoming winged adults. The adults are tiny, and it is easy to overlook them in the lawn.

Chinch bugs may be found throughout the season, depending on location. Their numbers may peak twice: in June and again in August. In warm climates, they may be active in winter.

They sometimes disappear suddenly. You could search a lawn a few days after first noticing damage and not find one.

■ *Control:* Chinch bugs are surface feeders and are easily controlled if diagnosed early. If you suspect chinch bugs, get down on your hands and knees and pull back the grass. You might see red nymphs scurry about near the base of the plants.

Granular and liquid insecticides are labeled for chinch bug control. Mow and water the lawn before spraying a control, applying ½ to 1 inch of water to bring the insects to the surface.

CHINCH BUG SYMPTOMS
■ In sunny areas and along pavement, the grass wilts, turns yellowish brown, dries out, and dies.
■ Damaged areas often outline the shade pattern of trees in the lawn.
■ When the grass is pulled back in a sunny spot at the edge of an affected area, you may see tiny reddish nymphs.
■ Various species found in all of North America

GREENBUG APHIDS

Greenbug aphids damage by sucking juices from leaf blades. The insects are tiny and often overlooked. Because they cause a bronze discoloration, homeowners frequently water the area, thinking the damage is from drought. Examining leaf blades with a hand lens is the best way to identify greenbug aphids as the problem. Look for tiny green bugs.

In northern regions the eggs survive over winter and hatch in spring; adults may also arrive in spring on winds blowing from southern regions.

GREENBUG APHID SYMPTOMS
■ Bronze discoloration; looks like drought damage.
■ Discolored areas usually develop in shaded spots under trees but can appear in sunny areas.
■ Primarily in the Midwest but possible in all of North America

Adults reproduce rapidly all summer and can increase to large numbers. They damage lawns throughout the Midwest and the East and have been observed in California.

■ *Control:* Greenbug aphids are surface feeders and are easily controlled with standard insecticides once they are identified.

SCALE INSECTS

Scale insects are related to aphids and feed like them, by sucking plant juices. Their feeding causes the lawn to yellow, as if damaged by drought. Scale insects move around during their first growth stage, when they look like tiny, almost microscopic aphids. Later, they settle in one location, secreting a white waxy shell to enclose their bodies.

Bermudagrass scales settle down near the base of the plant or on stolons. The scales are tiny, only 1/16 inch long, and shaped like clam-shells. Large numbers of them cause a moldy whitish look on the stems and crowns of the plants.

Ground pearls are also scale insects. The "pearls" are actually their waxy shell. They secrete a spherical shell as they feed on centipedegrass, bermudagrass, zoysiagrass, and St. Augustinegrass in the Southeast and the Southwest. Their feeding causes the grass to turn yellow, then die by fall.

■ *Control:* No pesticides are labeled for control of scale insects of lawns, although the insects might be controlled by insecticides applied for other pests. The best defense is to keep your lawn growing vigorously.

BERMUDAGRASS MITE SYMPTOMS
■ In spring, areas of a bermudagrass lawn fail to begin normal growth, remaining yellow or brown.
■ Swollen leaf sheaths form tufts or rosettes that turn yellow, then brown, then die.
■ Large clumps of distorted stems die; grass loses vigor and thins, allowing weeds to enter.
■ When one of the rosettes is shaken over a sheet of dark paper, nearly microscopic specks, smaller than grains of pepper, drop to the paper and begin to crawl around.
■ Mainly in the South and the Southwest

BERMUDAGRASS SCALE SYMPTOMS
■ In late summer, irregular patches turn yellow, then brown. The grass in the affected area may die.
■ Grass appears as if damaged from drought.
■ Look for hard white bumps on the grass stems, especially on or near the base of the plant.
■ Mainly a pest in the South and the Southwest

GROUND PEARL SYMPTOMS
■ During dry periods, irregularly shaped patches of grass turn yellow, then brown, then die in fall.
■ Among the roots in these patches can be found yellow-brown spheres that look like pearls and range in size from a grain of sand to 1/16 inch in diameter.
■ Southern states, especially Florida

Disease and controls

Diseases are caused by both living and nonliving factors. Nonliving factors, which include nutritional imbalances and drought, weaken plants, allowing living disease agents to move in. Among the living disease-causing organisms are bacteria, fungi, viruses, phytoplasmas, parasitic plants, and nematodes. Prevention is the best disease control you can employ.

Yellowing and thinning turf are symptoms of lawn diseases, insect pests, poor care, and many other problems. Take care to identify the cause so that you can apply the correct control.

PREVENTING LAWN DISEASES

The most important principle of preventing lawn diseases is to keep the grass healthy. Although plants have evolved chemical and physical defenses against diseases, they need energy to deploy them. The vigor they get from good care is your first and most important line of defense. Mow, water, and fertilize to optimize the growth and health of your lawn.

■ *Irrigating:* Many fungal diseases infect plants only when moisture abounds. If grass blades are wet for long periods or you water daily so the soil never dries out, your lawn is more likely to be infected. Follow the rules laid out in the chapter on watering, which starts on page 15: Water properly (at least ½ inch twice a week) in the early morning so that grass blades dry during the day.

■ *Mowing:* Mowing helps further the spread of some diseases by wounding the grass, giving pathogens easy points of entry into the leaf. Routinely mowing too short

Identifying lawn diseases

Diseases can be difficult to identify. Many, especially the patch diseases, look much the same. And from a distance, the symptoms of many diseases resemble those caused by poor lawn care practices or insect damage. The yellow area in your bluegrass lawn could be caused by a disease, an insect, or by hot weather.

■ **Make careful observations:** Look for distinctly shaped patterns in a lawn or lesions and spots on the leaf blades. The color and shape of spots in the lawn and on the blades hold clues to the disease. The disease profiles starting on page 72 describe the signs and symptoms for each disease.

■ **Get help from your local extension service:** Extension service staff will supply directions for collecting and delivering a sample of diseased grass. Usually you need to take one or more grass plants from the edge of the damaged area, where the fungus is most active. You'll probably also need to get some of the root and soil with the plant. Put the sample in a plastic bag and deliver it to the office rather than mailing it. The staff will likely culture the disease in a laboratory, so getting a definite identification may take several weeks.

weakens the grass, making it susceptible to infection. Lawns are healthiest when no more than a third of the blade is cut off at a time.

■ *Fertilizing:* Unlike most other plants, grasses have the ability to store excess nitrogen in their tissues. To pathogens, a healthy grass blade looks like a bank full of money waiting to be robbed. On the other hand, nitrogen deficiency weakens grass, leaving it open to infection. Managing your lawn's nutrition is an important step in preventing many diseases. Follow a balanced fertilizer program for your type of grass to keep the lawn healthy without promoting disease (see Fertilizing, page 7).

■ *Turfgrass selection:* You probably already have a lawn and must deal with whatever grass is growing there. If it is susceptible to disease and breaks out in spots every year, consider renovating it. That involves killing the existing grass and replanting with a better variety. When renovating or installing a lawn, your local extension service can recommend turfgrasses for your area.

■ *Thatch and aeration:* Thatch is a breeding ground for pathogens. Take the steps described in the chapter on managing thatch (page 33) to prevent thatch from growing thicker than ½ inch. Aerate to reduce thatch, relieve compaction, and improve drainage—all conditions that favor disease.

■ *Drainage:* Because it's difficult to improve drainage after a lawn is in place, it's important to do so before installing the lawn.

■ *Soil pH:* In many regions, you know if your soil is naturally acid or alkaline. Applying lime or sulfur every few years is a normal practice. However, pH is not so clear-cut in some regions. To ensure that the lime or sulfur you apply is needed, test your soil every few years.

Mow often enough to never remove more than one-third of the blade at a time. Begin mowing as soon as the lawn greens up in spring. Bag clippings when diseases are active to prevent infection.

FERTILIZING GUIDELINES

■ Aim for steady, season-long growth.

■ Feed 3 to 5 times per year, depending on the grass and region.

■ Use a fertilizer formulated for lawns.

FUNGICIDES

Diseases in home lawns rarely require fungicide treatment. They should be controlled with cultural techniques whenever possible, but situations may arise where it's necessary to use fungicides. Fungicides are chemicals that kill fungi or prevent spores from germinating. They are available in granules, liquids, and wettable powders.

Select a fungicide labeled for the disease, then apply it following all the directions on the label. Fungicides are more effective at preventing disease than curing it, so it's important to apply them at the right time. Refer to the disease profiles that follow to schedule fungicide applications when they will be most effective.

Disease profiles

LEAF SPOTS

The term *leaf spot* refers to several fungal diseases that form lesions on grass blades. One, melting-out caused by *Bipolaris sorokiniana,* is the most common. It affects cool-season grasses and bermudagrass but is especially destructive to common Kentucky bluegrass. Most improved grass varieties resist these diseases.

Lesions form on blades in cool spring and fall weather but may be seen any time of year. When the weather warms, the fungus kills the blades, spreads to the base of the plant, and kills entire plants. Lawns that are excessively lush from quick-release nitrogen fertilization or are under stress from short mowing, thick thatch, and over- or underwatering are most susceptible.

■ *Immediate control:* Apply a contact fungicide when leaf spotting is first noticed. Make at least three more applications, 7 to 10 days apart.

■ *Prevention:* Keep your lawn healthy and vigorous. Mow at the proper height and control excess thatch. Avoid overfertilizing. Water thoroughly once or twice a week. Try to keep the grass dry at night; do not water in late afternoon or early evening. When establishing a new Kentucky bluegrass lawn or reseeding an existing one, use improved cultivars that are resistant to leaf spot.

MELTING-OUT LEAF SPOT SYMPTOMS

■ From spring until fall, the grass turns light brown, dark brown, or reddish brown in irregular patches 2 or more feet across.

■ The grass in the patches thins.

■ In cool spring and fall weather, grass blades (both green and brown ones) have small oval spots with straw-colored centers and dark maroon to black borders.

■ As the summer warms, leaves and sheaths may be covered with spots, and entire plants may die.

■ North America

DOLLAR SPOT

Dollar spot is caused by the *Sclerotinia homeocarpa* fungus. On golf greens the blighted areas start out the size of a silver dollar. On home lawns, they are more often softball size. Spots can merge to form large, blighted areas. Active during moist, mild days and cool nights, dollar spot occurs in spring and fall. Infections may linger through the summer.

The disease is most severe on Kentucky bluegrass, bentgrass, and bermudagrass but may also attack bahiagrass, zoysiagrass, fescue, and ryegrass lawns. It usually attacks lawns that are under stress from lack of moisture or low fertility. Excess thatch may also contribute to an attack of dollar spot. An infection seldom damages permanently, although the lawn can take several weeks or months to recover. Dollar spot can be spread on the shoes of people walking over the lawn and by hoses, mowers, and other equipment.

■ *Immediate control:* Make two fungicide applications 7 to 10 days apart, beginning when the disease is first evident. Grass recovers quickly if treated promptly.

■ *Prevention:* Maintain proper nutrient levels. Applying fertilizer helps the lawn recover if it is nutrient-deficient. Control excess thatch. Water only in the morning, one or two times per week.

PINK SNOW MOLD

Also known as fusarium patch, pink snow mold is caused by *Michrodochium nivale,* a fungus. It develops in wet, cool (below 45°F) weather, and can be destructive under snow, particularly if the grass was still growing when snow first arrived.

Pink snow mold is most likely to occur after snow has been on the ground for several months or after prolonged rainy periods. Prolonged cold worsens symptoms; turf recovers quickly if warm weather follows snow melt. Serious infection leads to crown and root rot. Pink snow mold primarily affects cool-season grasses, although it may attack bermudagrass and zoysiagrass if conditions are right.

■ *Immediate control:* For seriously affected areas, apply a fungicide labeled for pink snow mold according to directions. Lightly infected turf usually recovers on its own. To encourage recovery, rake matted spots in early spring to improve air circulation to grass plant crowns.

■ *Prevention:* Reduce shade in affected areas. Avoid excess fertilizer in fall. Mow until the grass stops growing; overly tall grass is susceptible to pink snow mold. Reduce thatch buildup.

DOLLAR SPOT SYMPTOMS

■ During warm, wet weather in May and June and September and October, the grass turns light brown in circular areas, from the size of a silver dollar to 6 inches in diameter.

■ The spots may merge to form large, irregular patches several feet wide.

■ Small, light brown blotches the shape of an hourglass girdle the leaf blade. The blotches are tan in the middle with a reddish-brown halo above and below. The leaf tip may remain green, or the entire leaf blade may be blighted.

■ In the early morning before the dew dries, a cobwebby white growth may cover infected blades.

■ North America

PINK SNOW MOLD SYMPTOMS

■ Cool, wet weather favors this disease, especially after snow melts in spring.

■ Circular yellow-green spots a few inches in diameter. Grow to 6 to 12 inches in diameter and turn pinkish white. Patches may join together.

■ Affected blades are matted and light tan.

■ Patches grow outward with a rusty pink border.

■ Leaf blades do not have leathery, raised dots.

■ Northern states, the Pacific Northwest especially

Disease profiles

continued

GRAY SNOW MOLD

Also called typhula blight, gray snow mold is caused by *Typhula* fungi. Active only in cool (30° to 40°F), moist weather, gray snow mold is most likely when snow lasts for several months. Like pink snow mold, it grows under snow, but may continue to grow after snow melts. Prolonged cold weather worsens symptoms; turf recovers quickly when warm weather arrives. Gray snow mold primarily affects cool-season grasses.

■ ***Immediate control:*** For serious infections, treat with a fungicide labeled for the disease. (Generally, it is different from what is labeled for pink snow mold.) Rake dead patches thoroughly, then reseed them. Lightly infected turf usually recovers on its own.

■ ***Prevention:*** Do not apply excess quick-release nitrogen in early fall as grass goes into dormancy. Once grass is dormant, it's OK to fertilize. Rake and remove leaves before snow falls. Mow until the grass stops growing in fall; tall grass is most susceptible. Reduce thatch.

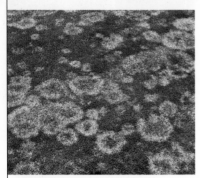

GRAY SNOW MOLD SYMPTOMS

■ **Yellow-green spots a few inches in diameter appear in cold, wet weather.**

■ **Spots grow in size and become covered with grayish-white mycelia.**

■ **Affected grass is matted and turns light tan.**

■ **Circular patches grow outward with a gray-white border.**

■ **Patches reach 2 feet in diameter and eventually join together.**

■ **Look for leathery, raised dots (sclerotia) on affected grass blades. The dots may be half the width of the blade.**

■ **Northern states**

YELLOW PATCH

Yellow patch appears in early spring as the lawn is emerging from dormancy. *Rhizoctonia cerealis,* the fungus that causes it, is especially destructive to Kentucky bluegrass and creeping bentgrass, but it can attack most cool-season grasses, including tall fescue

YELLOW PATCH SYMPTOMS

■ **Symptoms develop in early spring, as the lawn breaks dormancy.**

■ **Irregular, circular, light green to yellow-green patches start out 2 to 3 inches across and may grow to 3 feet in diameter.**

■ **Patches may have a frog-eye pattern.**

■ **Patches are distinctly sunken.**

■ **Diseased blades develop tan lesions with dark brown borders that eventually fade to tan.**

■ **A reddish-purple tint on the outer edge of the patch is possible.**

■ **Symptoms most obvious on closely mown turf.**

■ **North central and eastern states, the West Coast**

and perennial ryegrass, as well as bermudagrass and zoysiagrass. Affected warm-season grasses turn yellow for several weeks but usually recover. Wet weather between 40° and 60°F favors yellow patch. Symptoms disappear when temperatures are below 40°F or above 75°F. Yellow patch is easily mistaken for necrotic ring spot.

■ *Immediate control:* Apply fungicide labeled for yellow patch. In severe cases, renovate the lawn, resowing a resistant grass variety in affected areas.

■ *Prevention:* A balanced fertilizer program and proper management steps to reduce thatch will help with prevention and recovery from damage once it has occurred.

POWDERY MILDEW

Powdery mildew is caused by the fungus *Erysiphe graminis*. It occurs when the nights are cool (65° to 70°F) and damp and the days warm and humid. It is most severe on Kentucky bluegrass but also attacks bermudagrass and fescues. Shaded lawns are most affected, although the disease may be observed in open areas during extended wet, overcast conditions.

The disease is more unsightly than damaging. It slows the growth of blades, roots, and underground stems, causing gradual weakening and thinning of the grass and making the grass more susceptible to other problems. Some cultivars are highly susceptible, and in shade, the disease readily thins them out. Excessively fertilized, rapidly growing lawns are very susceptible to attack from this fungus. The fine white mildew on the blades develops into powdery spores that spread easily in the wind.

■ *Immediate control:* Treat the lawn with fungicide when mildew is first seen. Remember powdery mildew is rarely damaging; treat it only for appearance reasons.

■ *Prevention:* Reduce the shade and improve air circulation by pruning surrounding trees and shrubs. Fertilize and irrigate only moderately in shaded areas. If the grass is badly thinned by powdery mildew in shaded areas, reseed the area with species and cultivars better adapted to shaded conditions, such as fine fescue.

POWDERY MILDEW SYMPTOMS

■ Appears in cool, rainy weather, especially in shady areas

■ Whitish-gray mold is found on upper blade surfaces.

■ Lawn looks as if dusted with flour.

■ Leaf tissue under the mold turns yellow, then tan or brown.

■ Severely infected plants may wither and die.

■ North America, especially the Northeast and the Pacific Northwest

Disease profiles

continued

RUST

Rust forms an easy-to-rub-off, powdery orange-brown growth on the surface of grass blades. It occurs on most cool- and warm-season grasses, although it most frequently attacks Kentucky bluegrass, ryegrass, tall fescue, and zoysiagrass. The disease develops in summer and persists into fall. Moist, warm weather (70° to 75°F) and heavy dew favor its development. In areas with mild winters, it can appear in late summer or early fall and be active all winter.

Grasses under stress from nitrogen deficiency or lack of moisture are most susceptible to attack. Lawns severely attacked by rust are more likely to suffer winter damage.

■ *Immediate control:* If the disease is severe, treat with fungicide. Repeat the application every 7 to 14 days until the lawn improves. Because rust is a low-nitrogen disease, fertilizing helps the lawn recover.

■ *Prevention:* Rust develops slowly, often more slowly than the grass grows. Fertilize routinely to maintain rapid growth. Mow frequently and remove the clippings or use mulching mower blades to dice them up.

RUST SYMPTOMS
- Lawn turns orange-yellow or reddish brown and thins out.
- Rusty orange powder coats blades, rubs off on fingers, shoes, and clothing.
- Color comes from reddish-brown lesions on blades.
- North America, except the Southwest

BROWN PATCH

Brown patch is caused by the fungus *Rhizoctonia solani* and is sometimes called rhizoctonia blight. Affected lawns develop large, blighted patches that often have dark halos around them in the morning.

It is one of the most prevalent diseases in warm, humid areas, attacking all types of grass. It is common on Kentucky bluegrass in the Midwest and the East and can devastate tall fescue lawns during hot summers. It affects St. Augustinegrass in Florida, Texas, and along the Gulf

BROWN PATCH SYMPTOMS
- Circular patches of dead grass, a few inches to a few feet across, appear during periods of high humidity and warm (75°–85°F) temperatures.
- Dark gray, purplish, or black "halos" may surround the brown patches at night and persist into early morning.
- After 2 to 3 weeks, the brown grass in the center may recover and turn green, giving the patch a donut or frog-eye shape.
- Primarily east of the Rockies

Coast. Damage may show up late in the season and continue into fall. The halo pattern usually does not occur on St. Augustinegrass, but the fungus may move quickly and blight large sections of the lawn.

Lush, tender growth from using quick-release nitrogen fertilizer is most susceptible. Sometimes only the blades are affected, and the grass recovers in two to three weeks. When infection is severe and warm weather continues, the disease attacks plant crowns and kills the grass.

■ *Immediate control:* Control brown patch with fungicide. Treat when the disease is first noticed and at least three more times at 7- to 10-day intervals. Repeat the treatments as long as warm, humid weather continues.

■ *Prevention:* Keep grass as dry as possible to slow spread; water properly (one or two times per week) only in the morning. To reduce recurring infections, control thatch and follow a balanced fertilizer program. The heaviest feeding for cool-season grasses should be in late summer and fall rather than spring and early summer.

SUMMER PATCH

Summer patch *(Magnaporthe poae)* infects grass roots during cool weather (60° to 65°F), usually in late spring. Symptoms then appear from June through September, when hot, dry weather follows a wet period. When hot weather arrives, the roots cannot provide enough water, and the grass blades die.

The disease is most prevalent in compacted soil and lawns with excessive thatch, especially on exposed sites and steep slopes. It is worsened by quick-release nitrogen applications and, unlike most other diseases, by infrequent watering. It can affect many types of grasses, including bentgrass, Kentucky bluegrass, and fescue—especially when cultivars are unsuitable for local conditions. The symptoms of summer patch are so similar to those of necrotic ring spot that the two diseases cannot readily be distinguished without culturing them in a lab.

■ *Immediate control:* Apply fungicide to infected areas, following label directions. Reseed seriously affected areas with resistant grasses adapted to your climate. Once this disease has developed, it may take several months for complete recovery.

■ *Prevention:* Any cultural practices that help minimize thatch help prevent summer patch, as does using a balanced fertilization program. Light watering to prevent the thatch layer from becoming dry will help prevent initial development of the disease. Aerate and dethatch summer-patch-prone lawns yearly to prevent an outbreak.

SUMMER PATCH SYMPTOMS

■ Symptoms appear in hot summer weather.

■ Scattered patches of dead turf are 4 to 8 inches across (may grow as large as 1 to 2 feet across).

■ Patches are usually circular or crescent-shaped and occasionally are serpentine.

■ Frog-eye pattern develops.

■ If hot weather persists, the center of patch dies.

■ The patches may grow together and blight large sections of lawn.

■ Northeastern and north central states

Disease profiles

continued

Pythium blight symptoms
- Irregular ½- to 4-inch spots of wilted, shriveled, light brown grass develop in hot, humid weather from April to October.
- The spots enlarge rapidly to 1-foot-wide or wider streaks or 1- to 10-foot patches.
- Infected blades mat together when walked on.
- Cottony, cobweblike white threads bind blades in the early morning before the dew dries.
- Grass sometimes dies within 24 hours.
- Mainly cool-season grass regions

PYTHIUM BLIGHT

Pythium blight, also called grease spot or cottony blight, attacks heat-stressed lawns when temperatures are above 85°F. Poorly drained soil, excessive moisture, and low mowing also promote it.

Pythium blight is one of the worst diseases on golf courses, where it can kill the dense, lush, closely mown grass overnight. It is rarely that bad on home lawns, which generally have taller grass.

All cool-season turfgrasses are affected, with ryegrass the most susceptible. It can also attack bermudagrass under the right conditions. The fungus spores spread easily in free-flowing water, on lawn mower wheels, and on the soles of shoes. The disease is difficult to control because it spreads so rapidly, killing large areas in hours. Pythium blight is common in fall on winter-overseeded ryegrass.

■ *Immediate control:* Keep traffic off the diseased area to avoid spreading spores. Treat the lawn during hot, humid weather with a contact fungicide labeled for use on pythium blight as soon as the disease is noticed. Repeat treatments every 5 to 10 days until either the disease stops or cooler weather resumes. Severely infected areas often do not recover, and you will need to reestablish the lawn. Wait until cool weather to overseed.

■ *Prevention:* Don't overwater. Improve drainage. Mow at the highest setting possible. Follow a moderate fertilization program. Control thatch.

RED THREAD

Red thread *(Laetisaria fuciformis)* is most serious on fine fescue and perennial ryegrass lawns, but bentgrass, Kentucky bluegrass, and bermudagrass are also susceptible. It attacks only leaves and leaf sheaths and is seldom serious enough to kill a lawn. The disease is most active in cool, wet weather. Slow-growing, nitrogen-deficient lawns are most severely affected. Potassium deficiency may also make lawns more susceptible to attack.

■ *Immediate control:* If the weather conditions that favor the disease continue and the disease worsens, treat the lawn with a contact fungicide. Repeat the treatment two times at intervals of 7 to 10 days.

■ *Prevention:* Fertilizing with nitrogen and potassium may improve mildly diseased lawns.

ST. AUGUSTINEGRASS DECLINE (SAD)

Little is known about the spread of SAD except that it is caused by panicum mosaic virus. Like many viruses, it can be carried by insects that suck sap from infected plants and then transmit SAD to the next grass they feed on. The disease also spreads to healthy turf from infected grass clippings. Affected leaf blades develop a mottled yellow appearance that may spread over large sections of the lawn. Centipedegrass may also be susceptible to the disease.

■ *Immediate control:* There are no chemical controls and most cultural practices provide little relief once the disease has developed.

■ *Prevention:* Replace infected grass and a few inches of topsoil. Replant with grasses known to have some resistance to SAD, such as 'DelMar', 'Floratam', and 'Raleigh' St. Augustinegrass. Avoid cutting a healthy lawn with a mower that has recently trimmed an infected one. Do not mow wet turf.

Red thread symptoms
■ Grass turns light tan to pink in 2- to 36-inch, round patches, which appear in cool, wet weather.
■ Pink webs bind grass blades.
■ As blades dry, ¼- to ¾-inch-long pink threads protrude from tips.
■ Patches may grow together to blight large areas of the lawn if cool, wet weather continues.
■ All but southern regions

St. Augustinegrass decline symptoms
■ In the first year after planting, the lawn grows poorly and looks weak for no apparent reason.
■ Leaf blades have pale green spots, blotches, and stippling. Pale green mottling eventually appears.
■ Symptoms mimic those of iron deficiency or mite damage.
■ In the second year, grass may be bright yellow and stunted and become thin. Large patches of grass die.
■ Diseased plants may die before the third season.
■ The Gulf Coast

Other damage

CHEMICAL SPILL DAMAGE

SALT AND FERTILIZER DAMAGE

DOG DAMAGE

CHEMICAL SPILLS

Pesticides, gasoline, hydrated lime, and fertilizer may burn grass if overapplied or accidentally spilled. Excessive amounts of these materials cause leaf blades to dry out and die. Gasoline "sterilizes" the soil and prevents anything from growing in the area of the spill for years.

■ *Immediate control:* Prevent or minimize damage by immediately scooping or soaking up as much of the spilled material as possible and then flushing the chemical through the soil. If the substance is water-soluble, irrigate thoroughly—three to five times longer than usual. If the substance is water-insoluble—gasoline or oil, for example—flood the area with dish soap diluted in water to about the same strength as used for washing dishes. Then irrigate thoroughly as above. If the spilled material is a granule, pick it up with a wet-dry vacuum. Some substances, such as preemergence herbicides, cannot be washed from soil. In such a case, replace the top several inches of soil in the spill area.

■ *Prevention:* Fill gas tanks, spreaders, and sprayers on a hard surface, such as a concrete driveway. Apply chemicals according to label instructions.

SALT AND FERTILIZER DAMAGE

Salt desiccates plant tissue, drawing water out of the plant. The salt may come from materials put down to melt ice on sidewalks or be splashed from treated streets. In some areas, soil and water are naturally salty. Because fertilizer is made up of chemical salts, overfertilizing or spilling fertilizer results in the same symptoms.

■ *Immediate control:* Wash the salts through the soil with water. If damage occurs only in a low spot with poor drainage, fill it in.

■ *Prevention:* Fertilize properly according to label directions. Grow a salt-tolerant grass species.

DOG DAMAGE

Dog urine burns grass. The salts in the urine cause varying stages of damage, from slight discoloration to outright death. The nitrogen in the urine may encourage immediately surrounding grass to grow rapidly, resulting in a vigorously growing, dark green ring around the damaged area. Lawns suffer the most damage in hot, dry weather.

■ *Immediate control:* Mow high. Water affected areas thoroughly to wash away the urine. This reduces but does not eradicate the brown discoloration.

■ *Prevention:* Keep dogs off the grass, if you can. Train the dog to go to one section of the lawn. Consider getting a smaller dog or buying a home with a bigger lawn.

Reviving your lawn

Reviving basics

Buying a home with a neglected lawn. Not having enough time on weekends to do more than shuttle kids from their soccer game to their dance lesson. Summer-long drought. There are many reasons why lawns deteriorate and stay that way. Once you unpack and settle in, the kids head off to college, the drought ends, and you're ready for a new look, this chapter will help you get your lawn back in shape. In most instances, you'll find that it's remarkably easy. A little fertilizer and water, and you're back in business. Where it's not that simple, the following pages will walk you through the steps of reviving your lawn.

A REVIVING EXPERIENCE

Exactly how you improve your lawn depends upon your assessment of the current situation and, to a degree, upon your own standards.

■ ***Repairing the lawn*** is partial renovation. It means sowing new seed or patching with sod but otherwise working with what you've got. Choose this route to reinvigorate a thin or weak lawn that is otherwise okay.

Seed or sod can be used to repair a lawn. To repair a lawn with seed, scalp or slice the old lawn so that the seed is in direct contact with soil. Water well. Repair a lawn with new sod by slicing away the old sod and leveling the area as necessary. Lay the new sod, abutting it to the nearby turf. Trim it as necessary with a heavy knife.

■ ***Renovation*** starts with killing all the weeds and grass in your lawn with a nonselective weed control and then sowing seeds. Renovate if a good weed-and-feed isn't enough to improve the lawn, or if you don't need to till amendments into the soil or grade the soil. Also, weak lawns that are more than 10 years old are good candidates for renovation. New, improved varieties are less susceptible to pests.

■ ***Reestablishment*** means starting over. It's stripping off existing sod—or whatever is left of it—then tilling and amending the soil as necessary, just as you would when installing a new lawn. You might have to take measures this drastic if the soil grade or drainage is wrong or if the soil needs lots of lime or sulfur tilled into it to correct the pH.

Fertilizer and water may be all it takes to improve your lawn. Where this is the case, lawns that are fertilized and watered for a year will be healthy and vigorous the next year.

TIME IT RIGHT

Timing is everything when renovating a lawn. Exact timing depends on your region and the type of grass you are planting. Renovate cool-season grasses in late August if you live in the North, September to mid-October in the mild-winter West, and early spring in the South.

Dealing with lawn damage caused by natural disasters

HURRICANE DAMAGE

After a hurricane, you'll find uprooted trees, standing water, and silt and mud deposits on the lawn. The worst damage may come from salt-laden seawater, which can be blown inland or carried in on a tidal surge.

REPAIRING THE DAMAGE

Remove all debris, mud, and silt covering the lawn. Then irrigate to wash away salts. If using water from a well, have it tested to be sure it's not contaminated with salt. Core aerate so that water and salts move through the soil. Applying gypsum helps remove the salts. Water frequently and deeply until you're sure all the salt is washed beyond the root zone.

FLOOD DAMAGE

Flooded lawns are likely to survive if:
- They are submerged for less than four days (best case) to six days.
- Temperatures are below 60°F during this period.
- The water is flowing, not stagnant, supplying grass roots with oxygen.
- Silt is 1 inch deep or less.
- No erosion occurs.
- In warm-season regions, the grass is bermudagrass or zoysiagrass.
- Petroleum products don't contaminate the soil.

REPAIRING THE DAMAGE

Remove debris. Core aerate to help dry out the soil surface and break up crusty soil. Hose off as much silt as possible. Break up remaining silt crust with a rake. Fertilize.

Reestablish the lawn if the grass has died. Remove as much of the silt as possible. Till the soil, taking care to mix flood deposits with the dead grass and soil and to break up the old sod layer. Replant with an improved grass variety.

DROUGHT DAMAGE

Grass is quite resilient. Even though it may appear dead after prolonged drought, it may simply be dormant.

REPAIRING THE DAMAGE

When watering restrictions end, water well. As the grass resumes growth, evaluate the extent of its injuries before taking action.

Repair, Renovate, or reestablish

Weedy, thin lawns can often be salvaged without having to start from scratch. It's surprising how easy it is to salvage some lawns. Often, it's simply a matter of fertilizing and watering on a regular schedule and mowing at the correct height.

The first step to a better lawn is to assess the extent of damage. That will give you an idea of how big the job is and what it involves. A few simple repairs may be all that's required, or you may need to start from scratch.

Evaluating the extent of the damage involves

determining what caused the lawn to deteriorate. Lawns go bad for many reasons: lack of care, disease or insect attack, poor drainage, thin topsoil, or growing an unadapted grass species, to name a few. Correcting the cultural and environmental problems must be part of the process. Otherwise, any improvements may suffer the same fate.

A lawn with only a few damaged patches, totaling less than 30 percent of the area, will require only simple repairs. Determine the cause of damage first, so you won't need to repeat repairs in the future.

EVALUATE THE LAWN

An easy first step in determining whether you need to repair, renovate, or reestablish is to fertilize the lawn. The most common reason lawns deteriorate is that they lack nutrients. If the soil is infertile, the longest a lawn can last without being fertilized is two seasons. After five years, it may look as though the only solution is to replace the lawn. Actually, such a lawn will respond quickly to fertilizer. The easiest way to find out whether fertilizing will work with your lawn is to try it.

Following label directions regarding timing and quantity, apply a good-quality lawn fertilizer. If broadleaf weeds are also a problem, apply a postemergence broadleaf weed control or use a weed-and-feed to save a step.

If the grass responds in two to four weeks with new, vigorous growth, make a resolution to give your lawn good care and follow an annual fertilizer program. But if it doesn't, look more deeply, starting with the soil, the key to a healthy, vigorous lawn.

■ **Soil:** Dig into the upper 6 inches of soil. Is there sufficient topsoil for proper rooting? Check its depth; there should be a minimum of 4 to 6 inches of topsoil. Send a soil sample to a laboratory for testing.

If more than 50 to 70 percent of a lawn is damaged, it will need to be renovated.

Be sure that rock and debris are not buried
in the topsoil by poking a long screwdriver into
problem spots. Although it may seem odd that
you might find debris in the soil, many building
contractors bury rock, brick, leftover stakes, and
other construction debris rather than haul it from
the construction site. Problems may not show up
for years. They first become apparent during dry
weather, when the grass over the buried material
wilts because its root system is restricted. Wooden
debris may lead to circles of mushrooms called fairy rings.

First, evaluate the
soil. Check the
depth and quality of
the topsoil.

Also watch for low areas where water stands after a rain
or heavy irrigation.

When surface drainage is poor or nonexistent,
or you want to replace the topsoil or add
amendments to it, you'll need to remove the
existing grass, regrade the site, and replant—
in other words, reestablish the lawn. Small areas of
buried debris can be dug up, the debris removed,
and the damaged areas patched.

Next, evaluate the
plants. Look closely
at the roots, noting
their depth and
health.

■ *Grass:* Try to determine the predominant type
of grass in the lawn. Many poor lawns are the
natural result of grass struggling to survive where it is
not adapted to the conditions on the site. If the grass is a
remnant of an old pasture grass, nothing can be done to
improve it, short of renovation. If the grass is a lawn grass,
such as Kentucky bluegrass, some fertilizer and a
little care may quickly restore it.

Many older lawns suffer because trees have
matured and now shade the grass. Or the lawns
were established with an older grass variety
developed before insect- and disease-resistant
varieties were available. Here again, renovation
is called for.

Also, try to identify
the grass species to
learn whether it will
tolerate site
conditions.

■ *Weeds:* Neglected lawns are likely to have a
variety of weeds. Knowing which ones thrive in
your lawn is important in determining a course of action.

Perennial broadleaf weeds such as dandelion and
plantain are easily controlled with a selective herbicide.
Annual grasses are more of a problem but can generally be
handled without killing the entire lawn. It is the perennial
grass weeds that are the hardest to eliminate. If they infest
a large part of your lawn, you will need to kill them (along
with the lawn they infest) with a nonselective herbicide,
then renovate the lawn.

The perennial grass weeds that cause the worst
problems in cool-season lawns are quackgrass, coarse tall
fescue, and smooth bromegrass. Those in warm-season
lawns are Johnsongrass and torpedo grass. All have
underground rhizomes that allow them to regrow even
after their tops are removed. For this reason, it is difficult
to eradicate these perennial thugs.

Patching
a lawn

For medium-sized spots—saucer-sized to a few feet across—patching is a viable repair method.

Products that combine seed, mulch, and fertilizer, such as PatchMaster, make it possible for you to put down seed at the right rate, keep it moist until it germinates, and meet the germinating grass's nutritional needs in one step.

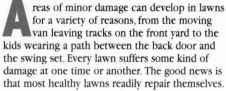

A reas of minor damage can develop in lawns for a variety of reasons, from the moving van leaving tracks on the front yard to the kids wearing a path between the back door and the swing set. Every lawn suffers some kind of damage at one time or another. The good news is that most healthy lawns readily repair themselves.

But sometimes a spot of dead or damaged grass is too large or too prominent to assume it will heal itself. And if you let it go, weeds have a nasty habit of creeping in. That's when you need to step in. With just a few basic techniques, you can repair the damage yourself, using seed, sod, sprigs, or plugs.

HOW-TO

The first step in patching the lawn is ensuring that the damage doesn't recur. You can assume a moving van won't be back for a while. But if the kids still play on the swing set, installing a path to it rather than patching the grass may be smart. Likewise, if damage resulted from insects and disease, you must take corrective action to ensure they won't damage the new grass.

Begin by squaring uneven sides and cutting away ragged edges from the damaged area. If soil needs to be brought in to raise up the level of the damaged area, be sure that it matches the existing soil. Major changes in soil type may result in growth variations due to moisture or fertility differences.

Adjust the soil level so that the finished patch matches the undamaged lawn surrounding it. If you will be seeding, sprigging, or plugging, bring the soil up to the level of the existing lawn. If you're going to use sod to patch the area, establish the new soil level about ½ to ¾ inch below the existing lawn grade.

The species and variety of grass used for the patch must match the existing lawn so the repaired area will not be visible. There is a surprising variation in the green color among the grasses. These color differences occur regardless of how much you fertilize, and simply fertilizing will not mask them. Textures also vary greatly, and may be readily apparent when combined.

After repairing the lawn, apply a starter fertilizer to the patched area. Follow up with an application over the entire lawn so that the patched area blends in quickly.

Take care when mowing a recently patched lawn. Riding mowers can damage the patches until they have matured. Sodded patches will stabilize in 10 to 14 days, whereas seeded patches may require several weeks before a mower can be operated over the area.

Making repairs

1 The steps for patching a lawn are fairly simple. They apply to whatever you use to patch with—seed, sod, stolons, or plugs.

First, square off the damaged area. This makes for a tidier patch. You'll also find it easier to cut a piece of sod to match the damaged area. Use a spade to do the work.

2 Rough up the soil surface. This helps seed, sod, plugs, or stolons make contact with the soil. If repairing tire tracks, loosen them with a fork. Insert the tines into the tracks and pull back. Bring in topsoil to raise the damaged area. When using sod, the soil level should be ¹⁄₂ to ³⁄₄ inch lower than the surrounding lawn.

3 Sprinkle seed or stolons over the prepared soil. Dig holes for plugs and insert them. Or cut a section of sod that roughly matches the size of the damaged area. Lay it on the prepared soil and finish trimming it to size. Use a heavy-duty pocket knife, an old butcher knife, or a small hatchet to do the cutting.

4 Make sure the seed, sod, stolons, or plugs make good contact with the soil. Press the area with the back of a garden rake.

5 Water the patched area thoroughly. Apply a starter fertilizer (follow label directions). Water in the fertilizer. Keep the patch moist until the seed germinates or the sod roots. To check rooting, tug on the sod. If it resists, its roots have begun to grow into the soil.

Renovating
a lawn

To renovate a lawn means to sow seed into the existing lawn after vigorously cultivating the soil with a power rake or slit-seeder. Renovating is much easier and less expensive than reestablishing the lawn because you don't grade, till, or do any of the other steps involved in installing a new lawn. Choose this solution when the soil is in good shape—loose, well-drained, and level—but the grass is in poor condition and cannot be salvaged by an annual fertilization program.

HOW TO RENOVATE

To eliminate perennial weeds, or to switch the lawn from an older, disease-prone grass species to an improved, better-adapted variety, spray a nonselective herbicide, such as glyphosate (Roundup®). It will kill most grasses and broadleaf plants. In addition, it is deactivated when it comes into contact with the soil, so it will not leave a residue that will damage germinating seedlings.

Where rhizomatous perennial grass weeds, such as smooth bromegrass, quackgrass, Johnsongrass, or torpedo grass, infest the old lawn, wait at least 10 days after spraying before planting, depending on the product you use. This allows time for the herbicide to move into the rhizomes and for you to ensure that they're dead.

With especially persistent weeds, it's a good idea to spray a second time 10 to 30 days after the initial application. Once existing vegetation is dead, scalp the grass, mowing it as low as possible. Set your mower to its lowest height ($\frac{1}{2}$ to $\frac{3}{4}$ inch). The goal is to leave a modest amount of dead grass to serve as a natural mulch and protect the new seedlings. However, it shouldn't be so tall that it blocks sunlight.

Next, cultivate the soil. Use a power rake—the same equipment used for dethatching—to further thin existing vegetation and expose the soil. The blades should reach through the thatch and slightly into the soil. Cutting through the old lawn and into the soil is an important step that ensures new seed makes contact with soil. Power rake the old lawn in one direction; then go back over it at a right angle. If your soil is heavy clay or seriously compacted, core-aerating at this stage is beneficial.

Next, apply the seed over the site. Then go over the lawn area one more time lightly with the power rake. Although it seems this might damage the seeds, it actually helps work them into the soil and improves germination. Finish with a final raking to smooth out uneven areas.

After seeding, make an application of starter fertilizer. Keep the seedbed moist until you can see the green of the new seedlings, gradually lengthening the time between waterings as roots establish and grow more deeply.

Renovation step-by-step

1 Kill existing lawn with a nonselective herbicide. Spray on a calm day, following all label directions. Be sure to apply the herbicide evenly, leaving no missed spots or strips.

2 Mow low, as low as ½ inch if your mower allows. This helps ensure the seed reaches the soil where it can germinate and take hold. The grass that remains provides a mulch for germinating seeds.

3 Cultivate the soil. Run a power rake over the grass, slicing through the thatch and into the soil *(left)*. If the soil is compacted, core-aerate to open it up *(right)*. Rake cores into holes (or use a slit-seeder; *see step 6*).

4 Sow the seed at the rate you would use when starting a new lawn on bare soil.

5 Rake in the seed or go over the lawn one more time with the power rake. This helps work the seed into the soil and improves germination. Finish with a final raking to smooth uneven areas; then apply starter fertilizer. Water well until the grass germinates and is tall enough to mow.

6 Where compaction is not a problem, use a slit-seeder to combine all these steps into one. It drops seed as it slices through the soil. Sow the seed in two passes: half in one direction, the other half at a right angle to the first. Finish by fertilizing and watering.

Reestablishing a lawn

Sod is a popular choice for quickly establishing a Kentucky bluegrass lawn.

The steps involved in reestablishing a lawn include: preparing and grading the soil, selecting a grass that matches the way you'll use your yard and that will grow well in your region, and installing it using the most appropriate method for the time of year and the type of grass you want to grow.

Seeding is the most popular method of planting simply because it is the easiest and least expensive. It also gives you a greater choice in varieties. However, not all grasses can or should be grown from seed. And if your time frame for establishing a lawn—the completion of your new home, for example—doesn't coincide with the best season for seeding, using sod will be better.

Bluegrass, ryegrass, and fescues grow easily from seed, so you are in luck if you live in an area where these cool-season grasses are adapted. Bluegrass can also be sodded.

Warm-season grasses are more often grown vegetatively—that is, planted through sodding, plugging, or sprigging. In the case of bermudagrass, the common types can be seeded, but most of the finer-textured hybrids must be grown vegetatively. Because they are hybrids, they don't grow from seed. Zoysiagrass seeds are slow to germinate, so it is often sodded or plugged. St. Augustinegrass is another species that can be established by seed but is more often grown from plugs or sod to take advantage of disease-resistant cultivars. Centipedegrass, bahiagrass, and buffalograss can also be established by either means.

GRASSES FOR SEEDING
- Bahiagrass
- Bluegrass
- Buffalograss
- Centipedegrass
- Common bermudagrass
- Fescue
- Ryegrass

GRASSES FOR SODDING
- Bahiagrass
- Bluegrass
- Buffalograss
- Centipedegrass
- Fescue
- Hybrid bermudagrass
- St. Augustinegrass
- Zoysiagrass

TIMING IS EVERYTHING

The beginning of the growing season is the ideal time for seeding either warm- or cool-season lawns. However, the growing season varies greatly between the two.

Warm-season grasses grow actively in summer, so spring and early summer are the best times for installing a warm-season lawn. Seed or sod them anytime from early spring on the Gulf Coast to June in the lower Midwest to the mid-Atlantic seaboard.

Cool-season grasses grow actively in fall and spring but may go semidormant in summer due to heat or drought stress. Late summer and early fall are the times when a newly seeded cool-season lawn can have both the moderate temperatures needed for germination and sufficient time for grass to grow.

In spring, it's better to sod cool-season lawns. You can seed them then, but you must control summer weeds such as crabgrass, goosegrass, and foxtail, which will overrun a new seeding when the weather turns hot. Late fall and winter are risky times to try to establish a lawn by seeding, especially in areas with freezing weather.

For more information on when to establish grasses in your area, contact your county extension office or a garden center. You can also call the Scotts help line (800-543-8873). Extension offices, located at universities in many states, will also have information on the Internet. Search the name of the university and the word extension. When you get to the site, link to information on the subject of lawn care.

Seeding vs. sodding

A 1,000-square-foot lawn (measuring 50 × 20 feet) costs less than $10 to plant Kentucky bluegrass seed and up to $200 to sod. All costs for site and soil preparation are basically equal.

DO IT YOURSELF?

To install a lawn yourself, you will need to rent and operate a tiller and be physically able to spread soil amendments and rake out the soil after tilling. All of this needs to be accomplished at the optimal planting time. Getting the soil ready for planting is hard work. For some people, it is part of the pleasure of owning a home; for others, it is the only affordable route to a new lawn. And for still others, it is not even a consideration.

Most landscapers have the tools, equipment, personnel, and knowledge to do the job right and quickly. If you decide to use a landscape contractor, start interviewing early. Dependable contractors are always stretched thin during busy gardening months. Be sure to check references before choosing a contractor, and stick with well-established firms.

Index

Note: Page numbers in
boldface type indicate
profile entries. All plants,
insects, and pathogens are
indexed by their common
names.

METRIC CONVERSIONS

U.S. Units to Metric Equivalents			Metric Units to U.S. Equivalents		
To Convert	Multiply By	To Get	To Convert	Multiply By	To Get
Inches	25.4	Millimeters	Millimeters	0.0394	Inches
Inches	2.54	Centimeters	Centimeters	0.3937	Inches
Feet	30.48	Centimeters	Centimeters	0.0328	Feet
Feet	0.3048	Meters	Meters	3.2808	Feet
Yards	0.9144	Meters	Meters	1.0936	Yards

To convert from degrees Fahrenheit (F) to degrees Celsius (C), first subtract 32, then multiply by $5/9$.

To convert from degrees Celsius to degrees Fahrenheit, multiply by $9/5$, then add 32.